I0152314

AN ABUSED MAN'S

BATTLES, TRYING TO

PROTECT HIS BOYS

PUBLISHING COMPANY

TABLE OF CONTENTS

JESSE

BRENDA

CORINNE

ADDITIONAL INFORMATION AND CONCLUSION

ABOUT THE AUTHOR

I graduated high school in 1977 from Oregon Trail High School, that's the first year Stanfield, Oregon and Echo, Oregon merged into one school district for a 'trial period'. After the two years the two school districts went back to being their separate school districts. For several years after 1977 I worked and went to Blue Mountain Community College in Pendleton, Oregon where I took a lot of General Studies and eventually I earned my Associate of Applied Science Degree in Diesel Technology. Later I went to Messenger College in Joplin, Missouri for a year and transferred to Lee University in Cleveland, Tennessee where in 1998 I earned my Bachelors Degree in Psychology and two minors, one in Counseling and one in Religion. I learned about Copyright Laws at City University in Vancouver, Washington where I studied for my Masters in Counseling of school children. At City University I also submitted my fingerprints to the Federal Bureau of Investigation for a background check. The Federal Bureau of Investigation would either 'accept' you or 'reject' you. The Federal Bureau of Investigation results came back 'ACCEPTABLE', this was long after I was divorced. In other words, I passed the Federal Bureau of Investigation background check for counseling school children. I never completed the studies at City University because once I mentioned Jesus and used Bible scriptures in one of my oral reports my grades dramatically fell from a 2.8, which my advisor told me could be easily made up the next semester, to less than a 1.0. What would you expect for a Christian in a Secular School. Now, the Washington Counseling Association, the American Counseling Association, and the Federal Bureau of Investigation said I was and still am 'QUALIFIED' for counseling and being around underage children, then how can Children's Protective Services allow a Convicted Child Molester and a victim of Child Molestation to be better parents than I am? Read this book and find out what happened. I guarantee you, if any of the accusations my ex's and the Psychology report that was done on me, PAID FOR BY WALLA WALLA COUNTY WASHINGTON was true, then I would never have been able to pass any of the qualifications that I passed for the Washington Counseling Association, the American Counseling Association, and the Federal Bureau of Investigation. I also have two separate letters from two separate Doctors of Psychology in Umatilla County Oregon who at two different times, years apart from each other, put in writing that I am a 'fit parent' and there is nothing wrong with me having any of my boys, the Doctors of Psychology are both Christians. One of whom worked for Umatilla County Mental Health in Umatilla County Oregon and saw me and my second ex, Brenda, in marriage counseling before I ever went to see him for the anger management.

INTRODUCTION

This book is about my battles with Children Protective Services in Walla Walla County Washington and Children Protective Services in Umatilla County Oregon trying to get my boys out of the custody of a man who is a **CONVICTED CHILD MOLESTER** and a woman who is a **VICTIM OF CHILD MOLESTATION**. The second section of this book has to be received separately from the first half of this book, the second half contains all the evidence that proves that everything in the first half of this book is 100% true. Yes, my boys are still in their custody at the time of this writing. This particular book is going to be different than the others I have written. One time my ex literally kidnapped the boys and the Umatilla County Children Protective Services and the Oregon State Police said there was NO REASON to interfere because I wasn't doing anything wrong, and my boys were in proper care. On another occasion my second ex wife, who was molested as a child for several years herself by her own brother, and her boyfriend who is a **CONVICTED CHILD MOLESTER** (not accused, but actually **CONVICTED of 'INDECENT LIBERTIES'**) from Thurston County Washington, that she later married actually took the boys while the boys were in Foster Care in Walla Walla County Washington over a state line to live with her new boyfriend at her brother's house (The same brother who molested her while she was a juvenile.) The case worker had to drive down to California to retrieve the boys before my next visitation and I still lost the boys. What my ex's and all the individuals and county and state agencies who helped them 'sweep things under the rug' didn't stop to think about is that this country boy would eventually get a Bachelor's Degree in Psychology, Minors in Counseling and Religion from an Accredited University and technology would advance so far from the 1980's to today, that I would not only be able to write a book about what happened to me and my boys, but also be able to publish the book with International Copyright Laws that legally protect me and this book, **WORLD WIDE**. Most of these events take place in Umatilla County Oregon and Walla Walla County Washington. The names in this half were changed to protect the guilty. The second half of this book called, 'AN ABUSED MAN'S BATTLES, TRYING TO PROTECT HIS BOYS- EVIDENCE SECTION can be found at www.crossover-ministries-publishing.com. The Evidence Half contains all the original documents. **THIS IS WHAT IT'S LIKE TO BE AN ABUSED MAN.**

BOOKS WRITTEN BY WALTER BURCHETT, BA:

MATTHEW'S WORD 'TWO':REAL WORD OF GOD BIBLE   ISBN: 1-4116-6995-9

HEAVENLY ANGEL LAY LAY EXPLAINS WHY ADAM WAS NEVER CURSED
                                        ISBN: 978-1-84728-176-0

HEAVENLY ANGEL LAY LAY EXPLAINS WHY ABORTED BABIES DO NOT GO TO HEAVEN
                                        ISBN: 978-0-6151-7470-9

HEAVENLY ANGEL LAY LAY EXPLAINS THE BIBLICAL GROUNDS FOR MARRIAGE,
      SEPARATION, AND DIVORCE   ISBN: 978-0-6151-7481-5

HEAVENLY ANGEL LAY LAY EXPLAINS WHY PROFESSIONAL COUNSELORS HAVE 'HARDENED
      HEARTS'   ISBN: 978-0-6151-7482-2

HEAVENLY ANGEL LAY LAY EXPLAINS THE DIFFERENCE BETWEEN A 'COLD CHRISTIAN' AND
      A 'BACKSLIDER'   ISBN: 978-0-6151-7483-9

HEAVENLY ANGEL LAY LAY EXPLAINS WHICH BIBLE TO READ, WHICH BIBLE NOT TO READ,
      AND WHY   ISBN: 978-0-6151-7484-6

HEAVENLY ANGEL LAY LAY EXPLAINS WHY GAYS, LESBIANS, BI-SEXUALS, AND
      TRANSSEXUALS DO NOT GO TO HEAVEN   ISBN: 978-0-6151-7485-3

HEAVENLY ANGEL LAY LAY EXPLAINS WHY CHILDREN AND SPORTS ARE DEFINITELY A
      RELIGION IN TODAY'S SOCIETY   ISBN: 978-0-6151-7486-0

HEAVENLY ANGEL LAY LAY EXPLAINS WHAT 'MANY ARE CALLED, BUT FEW ARE CHOSEN
      REALLY MEANS   ISBN: 978-0-6151-7487-7

HEAVENLY ANGEL LAY LAY AND GUARDIAN ANGEL SHADOW GUESS THE REAL AGE OF THE
      EARTH   ISBN: 978-0-6151-7488-4

AN ABUSED MAN'S BATTLES, TRYING TO PROTECT HIS BOYS   ISBN: 978-0-6151-5191-5

JESSE

JESSE AND I MEET

Jesse and I met at the Assemblies of God Church in Pendleton, OR in 1982. I remember it vividly because her sister, Rhonda, was serving pie and Jesse didn't like the kind of pie the church was serving so I asked Jesse if she wanted to go to a restaurant for a piece of pie, Jesse accepted. Rhonda had a Bachelor's Degree in Psychology by the time I met Jesse. Rhonda worked at Children's Services Division in Pendleton, Oregon. In the weeks to come Jesse and I fell in love with each other and went to church together. During that time my dad passed away, the only father I ever had, meaning I never had a step-father or adopted father so when I say 'dad', there was only one 'dad' in my life. Jesse went to his funeral and comforted me through that hard time in my life. That was before Jesse and I were ever married.

Jesse and I were married and Rhonda was the Maid of Honor. My sisters Marge, June, and Linda were all Brides Maids. Rhonda loved the 'spot light' and being 'in control', and being the Maid of Honor Rhonda wanted to 'stand out' from the Brides Maids, which was good, but almost equal to Jesse, which was not good. All the women in the wedding were going to have a ribbon in their hair, except Jesse. Rhonda cut the ribbon for her and all the Brides Maids the same. The problem was that Rhonda was going to be standing at a different angle than Marge, June, and Linda and no one really thought about that until the next morning. The angle the guests would see the hair of Rhonda was different than the angle the guests would see the hair of Marge, June, and Linda. In order for the guests to be able to see the ribbon in all the women on stage that were supposed to be seen and not take the 'spot light' off the Bride, Jesse, was to place the ribbon on the Brides Maids in a different location in their hair than the Maid of Honor and that meant the ribbon for the three Brides Maids had to be cut shorter than the ribbon for the Maid of Honor. The morning of the wedding Marge asked Jesses if Jesse wanted the ribbon in Rhonda's hair to be like the ribbons in my sisters hairs or if Jesse would prefer the ribbon in Rhonda's hair to be different. Rhonda, being the Maid of Honor, the different cut of the ribbons would make Rhonda stand out even more from the Brides Maids, but still not take the spot light off the Bride, which was good. Jesse thought it was a good idea and agreed. Marge cut the ribbons that were going to be in my sisters hairs different than Rhonda had cut the ribbons. The Brides Maids wore the ribbons in their hair differently than the Maid of Honor. Rhonda didn't know anything about this happening until it was time for the wedding and my sisters, the Brides Maids, walked on the stage of he wedding. Rhonda saw what happened and really got angry, right in the wedding service. Rhonda actually started toward Jesse and Marge got Rhonda's attention and said it was Jesse's wedding and told Rhonda to shut up. Rhonda got so angry she actually walked off the stage right when the pictures were to be taken and stayed in the bathroom with the door locked until after my best man literally left the service. You can tell just by looking at the wedding pictures Rhonda was still angry when the pictures were taken. Jesse was getting married to a man who loved her before Rhonda got married. How dare Jesse, the younger sister get married before Rhonda, the older sister, especially when Rhonda was literally left at the alter by some man.

    After Jesse and I were married, it was quite apparent that no one in her family wanted us to be married, especially Rhonda. It got to a point that every time Jesse and I would go to her mom and dad's house and Rhonda was there, no matter what I said to Jesse about what Jesse and I should do in our own family business Rhonda kept saying Jesus, did you know that's grounds for divorce? I didn't understand what Rhonda was doing at the time, but having a degree in Psychology, Rhonda did. What Rhonda was doing was planting seeds of doubt and divorce in Jesse's mind for Jesse to divorce me and Rhonda did it on purpose, remember Rhonda had a Bachelor's Degree in Psychology at that time. Rhonda understood how the conscious and subconscious mind worked and the words Rhonda said would stand out in Jesse's mind when there was friction between Jesse and myself. Eventually Jesse's subconscious mind would make Jesse act on Rhonda's words. After Jesse and I were married we moved around a few places and we both started working at the potato processing plant for J R Simplot Company in Hermiston, Oregon where McDonald's French Fries and other McDonald's products were made, along with a few Simplot potato products. When Jesse and I found out Jesse was pregnant with Jacob, my first son, we went over to her mom and dad's to tell them the good news. Jesse asked them how they felt about being an uncle, aunt, grandpa, or grandma all her family could say is they take it Jesse is pregnant. No congratulations, no hugs, no nothing. Then everyone went back to doing what they were doing before Jesse and I interrupted them. My family on the other hand congratulated us and started getting things together and helping us prepare for Jacob to come into our lives once we found out the baby was a boy. At that time Rhonda worked at the Children's Services Division in The Dalles, Oregon.

    Jesse worked until she couldn't work any longer due to her pregnancy. She actually stopped working two days before her maternity leave started, but no supervisor wrote her up for taking those two days off. Everyone working could tell Jesse shouldn't have been be at work during that last week Jesse showed up for work, it was all she could do to sit there. During that last spring we were together, I got a spring job at work instead of being laid off during at spring break. That would keep us with health insurance and at least some money for our rent, food, and bills. I worked in the Fab Shop, the Fabrication Shop was where the welders made machinery for the plant. After Jacob was born Jesse stayed at home and took care of him while I kept working. That summer I was fortunate enough to work in the Fab Ship again.

    One day I was able to get off work two hours early and went home. It was actually payday that day too, that means it was Friday. I was going home and surprise Jesse then go out and buy her a dozen roses. I got home and found a strange car in our driveway. I walked in the front door and saw Jesse come out of our bedroom with a strange man. She was buttoning up her shirt and he was zipping up his pants. The man quickly walked into our bathroom and came out a few minutes later. I walked in our bedroom and saw the covers pulled back and a big wet spot in the middle of our bed and one of her negligee's laying on the floor. Jesse quickly took the sheet and the rest of the bedding and put them in our washer. Jesse introduced me to the man as being an old high school classmate that got a job as a vacuum cleaner salesman. The vacuum was there, so I didn't doubt that. I just couldn't figure out how the big wet spot got on our bed. I peaked through the window when Jesse went with the man to his car and she gave him a hug and kissed him. I couldn't figure out why she hugged and kisses him. I was in denial for three years believing Jesse would never cheat on me. Every time I told someone, they said she cheated on me and I stuck up for her for three years saying no, she wouldn't to that, but I still cant figure out how that big wet spot got on the sheet in the middle of the bed. Jacob was in his crib at the time, about two months old, and his crib was in our bedroom.

About two weeks later I came home from work and caught Jesse and her family moving Jesse and Jacob out of our house. Jesse was leaving me and taking Jacob with her. Jesse wanted to go to Vancouver, Washington to our old minister and talk to him and his wife. This was the same minister who performed our wedding ceremony. Later I called Vancouver, Washington and talked to the minister and asked him what he and Jesse talked about, the minister said Jesse never showed up. Jesse went down to The Dalles, Oregon and stayed with her sister Rhonda instead. Now remember, Rhonda was jealous of Jesse and I ever getting married to begin with.

About two weeks later Jesse served me with a Restraining Order saying I abused her and Jacob. The reason for the abuse is Jacob had a Cheed Cheek. I didn't know what a Cheed Cheek was so I went up to the Pediatrician an asked him. The Pediatrician said a Cheed Cheek is when the infant's cheek gets a little red due to someone or something rubbing on the infant's cheek. In other words, I didn't shave close enough that morning or I shaved that morning and by the time evening came around I had a few whiskers on my cheeks when I lifted Jacob up and rubbed his cheek on mine giving him love, that made his cheek red, that's what a Cheed Cheek is. I went to an attorney and asked him what to do. The attorney said, just stay away from her and let the Restraining Order die, it's no big deal. Back then, Restraining Orders were only good for three to six months. If I had it to do again, I would have fought that one and won. Just after that Restraining Order died, I went up and wanted to see Jacob. Jesse wouldn't let me and put another Restraining Order on me, this time for one year. I did ask for a hearing for that Restraining Order, but had to do it myself because I couldn't afford an attorney, Jesse hired an attorney. The morning of my hearing mom had to work about ten minutes longer than usual, instead of getting off work at 8 AM and getting home at 8:15 AM, mom didn't get to the house until 8:25 AM. We went as fast as we could to Pendleton, Oregon twenty-five miles away, to the hearing. Back then the speed limit was only 55 Miles Per Hour we didn't have a second car, the only car I had Jesse got when she left. That meant I couldn't get from Stanfield, Oregon to Pendleton, Oregon where the hearing was until 9:07 AM and the hearing started at 9 AM. Yes, to this day I remember looking up at the court room clock and seeing the time being 9:07. I walked into the court room seven minutes late and the judge slammed down the gavel and walked out. The Restraining Order stayed on. Jesse's attorney advised me Jesse was going to file for a divorce. The divorce hearing came and I still couldn't hire an attorney. I had lost my job due to the stress and I lost Jacob too.

Later on I found myself living in a 1974 Datsun Pickup, sleeping in the back with a cheap piece of plywood over me trying to keep the rain out, it was spring and raining a lot. I had to park in an apartment parking lot. A couple of women from the Assemblies of God Church in Hermiston, Oregon who had teenagers, did what they could to feed me until they were criticized so much from the church members they finally told me I couldn't stay parked there any longer. (Let me tell you good Christian judges something right now. If you criticize anyone for that reason, shame on you. When someone is down and out like I was and there is someone in the church helping someone like that, who are you to say what Jesus does or doesn't like. The scripture don't distinguish between a man and a woman when it says, 'when you give to my child, you give to me.' If Jesus lays it on a woman's heart to help a man in that situation you leave that woman alone. You wouldn't condemn a man for helping a woman out so don't condemn a woman for helping a man out. You say it doesn't look good, well, building an ark in the middle of the desert with over one hundred degree weather for years on end doesn't look right either now does it, until the ark is needed. You are afraid something intimate may happen, right? Whether that does or doesn't happen, it's really none of your business, that's between those two and Jesus. Maybe Jesus brought them together that way, you don't know. In today's age, I'd rather see a woman helping a man than a man helping a man and a man helping a woman than a women helping a women. Why do I say that? God only knows how many gays and lesbians are in the churches today. You know exactly what I am going with that statement, don't you.)

Anyway, a man from the Assemblies of God Christian Singles who was going through his own divorce told me I could stay with him for a while. I stayed with him for over a year, rent free, I couldn't work, although I did look for work, my mental capabilities just weren't there. He later married a woman from the Seattle Washington area. During the time I stayed with him, I went to Dr. Alexander (Evidence Section Page 8), a Christian and private counselor I saw for over a year. Dr. Alexander finally said I was good enough to have Jacob unsupervised. As of March 1986 according to Dr. Alexander, I had far exceeded what the court wanted me to do, so I had to hire an attorney and take Jesse back to court. Another year rolled by and I won six weeks of supervised just for Jacob to get used to me because of his young age and then the supervised visits would revert to unsupervised visits automatically.

BRENDA

HOW BRENDA AND I MET

Brenda and I met on Valentines night. A few of my friends and I went to Shari's Restaurant in Hermiston, Oregon on Highway 395 for Valentines Dinner. My friends went through the door first and I was still at the outside door when all of a sudden I saw some woman running to the door with what looked like a baby blanket with something in it, she had an infant in her arms. It was raining that night so I waited and held the door open for her. We dated for a while, during our dating period I found out she wasn't a Christian. We started going to the Assemblies of God Church in Hermiston, Oregon and within a few months the conversation came up about a Christian marrying a non-Christian. I told her that I would never marry a non-Christian. A few weeks later she let me lead her in the Salvation Prayer and later we married, Brenda said the words just so I would marry her. Brenda was about 5'5" and weighed about 250 pounds and I was 5' 9" and weighed about 135 pounds.

When Brenda and I were first married we lived in a small two bedroom apartment in Pendleton, Oregon. That was good enough for us and Stevey, Brenda's son was named after his father from a previous relationship. Brenda was never married to Stevey's father. Stevey's father, Stephen, was later convicted of child molestation of his own infant daughter from a different woman and served time in the Umatilla County Jail in Pendleton, Oregon. Brenda met Jesse, my first ex-wife, when we were going back and forth from Pendleton, Oregon where we lived down to Bend, Oregon where Jesse lived. We put about a 1,000 miles a month on our car just going down to Bend, Oregon to see my first born son, not to mention all the tires we went through. We couldn't afford new tires so we had to settle for used ones.

Later, when we found out Brenda was pregnant with Jeff, we moved into a low-income two bedroom townhouse located at 294 South West 28th Drive in Pendleton, Oregon. We started going to marriage counseling with Mental Health in Pendleton, Oregon. Our marriage was like two women running our home. We had Jesse controlling when we could see Jacob and Brenda trying to fight back looking out for Stevey, I was caught in the middle of the two. This is when we first met Dr Jones (Evidence Page 198), even though he lived in Hermiston, Oregon, he went to Pendleton, Oregon one day a week to counsel for the Pendleton Branch of the Umatilla County Mental Health. One day during our counseling session Brenda got extremely angry with me and started hitting me on the right shoulder with her fists right in front of Dr Jones (To this day I even remember what shoulder she hit me on.). Brenda got up and left the counseling session before the session was even over, during this time I did call the Abuse Hotline for help. I was told that I was able to be put in a shelter, but there were a lot of women in the shelter who hated men and even though it was my choice they really couldn't guarantee my safety. So I had the choice to either stay with an abusive wife or go to an abuse shelter with a lot of women who may wind up hitting me as well.

One day Brenda and I got into an argument and all the counselors told me if you two start arguing and nothing is getting accomplished, just leave the house and take a break. Well, I did this time, we were upstairs in the hallway and there was a banister there. Brenda was definitely showing with Jeff, she had to have been in her second trimester. Brenda was between me and the downstairs stairwell, I went right around her down to the bottom floor and out the door, got in our car and took a drive. Last time I saw Brenda, she was still on the edge of the upstairs hallway crying for me to come back. I get back home and find out one of the neighbors took Brenda to Doctor Sheep's office in Pendleton, Oregon. When I got to Dr. Sheep's office I still didn't know what happened, all I knew was that Brenda was in pain and went to see the doctor. Dr. Sheep told me, 'I don't approve of what you did.' and I said, 'Don't worry, it'll never happen again.' I was assuming Dr. Sheep was talking about me leaving Brenda by herself when she was crying at the edge of the upstairs hallway and I left just like the counselors at Mental Health told me to do. I was going to tell the Mental Health Counselors their advice about walking away and leaving the situation didn't work and I wasn't going to do it again. It wasn't until after Brenda and I left Dr Sheep's office that Brenda told me she told Dr Sheep I pushed her down the stairs and then left the house. Brenda actually blamed me for pushing her down a flight of stairs while she was showing with Jeff and I wasn't even home.

Yes, the neighbor lady who took Brenda to Dr Sheep's Office knew I wasn't there, but where are neighbors when it comes time for court hearings? They have all moved away and no one even knows you will need them at the time they move because no papers have even been filed yet. At other times the neighbors take sides, or a Restraining Order is file and you can't even get to the neighbor's house because the neighbor's house is too close to the house you are ordered to stay away from, even ministers move before court hearings come around. I don't even remember the neighbor lady's name and never did, all I ever remembered was the neighbor lady's face. I would see her and we could talk and even with her telling me her name, before I left the conversation I would forget.

On June 29, 1989 Brenda served me with a Summons for Divorce (Evidence Section Page 10.). Well, I didn't fight it, I didn't need to. Brenda and Stevey started showing up at my mom's house, where I was living, almost before the Divorce Papers were even served on me, I moved back to Pendleton. Now if you notice the Summons was filed five months before Jeff was born, less than a week before the fourth of July. That separation lasted about a week before Brenda started looking me up.

My mom lived and still does live close to Main Street in Stanfield, OR, there was a tavern right beside mom's house called, The Alibi across the street from the Main Street Market in Stanfield, Oregon, since that time the tavern was sold a couple of times and has burned down. At the time, I was in the tavern playing pool, like a lot of small towns that's all there is to do.

All of a sudden I was told there was a phone call for me and it was Brenda,. I really wasn't that surprised because Brenda had served Restraining Orders on me for no reason before and always contacted me later. Brenda could contact me, but I wasn't allowed to contact or go around her, so I didn't. I might also add here that a Restraining Order was good for one year at that time, there were no three month or six month Restraining Orders. There was a Prison Guard in the tavern on her way home from work, the Prison Guard worked in Pendleton, Oregon at the State Penitentiary. The Prison Guard was still in her uniform and she over-heard me talking on the phone. She offered to go across the street to supervise me seeing Stevey and Brenda so I wouldn't get into any trouble since Brenda drove from Pendleton to Stanfield and called me.

We assumed that since the Prison Guard worked for the State of Oregon and worked at a Correctional Facility that everything was legal. The Prison Guard and I walked across Highway 395 to the Main Street Market and I visited with Stevey. All of a sudden, the Stanfield Police drove by and pulled into the Main Street Market Parking Lot.

The Prison Guard and I filled the Stanfield Police Officers in on what happened and the Stanfield Police Officers called 'our meeting' into the Hermiston Police Department Dispatch Center and took over the Supervision for the Visitation. We didn't know it until the Stanfield Police told us, but a Prison Guard doesn't have the legal authority to supervise a visitation because a Prison Guard doesn't have the authority or training to arrest anyone in case something does go wrong with the visitation. No one got in trouble since I had several witnesses stating Brenda did call me and offered the visitation, the Stanfield Police just wanted to clear up the assumption that a Prison Guard had the authority to supervise a visitation when they don't.

I had already put in a 'Request for a Hearing' in at the Umatilla County Court House in Pendleton, Oregon. The hearing date never came around because Brenda dropped the 'Restraining Order' the next day. I will tell you now and mention it a few more times in this book, during the time Brenda and I were together, which was about five years, she served me with five different Restraining Orders and dropped them all, until she had a new boyfriend in her life. The papers say about six years, that's because it takes almost a year for the divorce court and divorce papers to go through.

What Brenda did was serve me with a Restraining Order and then after she showed me she was going to be in control of everything she would go up to the Pendleton Court House and sign another legal paper asking the judge to drop the Restraining Order. Every time the judge would sign an order to Restrain me and within two weeks the judge would sign another paper to drop the Restraining Order. There was never any hearing because the Restraining Order was always dropped before the Hearing Date came up, that's how Brenda was able to serve me with five different Restraining Orders in less than four years. Brenda and I were married for about a year before the first Restraining Order was ever filed. If you stop and think about it, it's impossible to serve and win a hearing for five different Restraining Orders, each Restraining Order lasting a whole year from the time the 'Temporary Restraining Order' was first served to the time the last 'Permanent Restraining Order' runs the length of a whole year. The Restraining Orders back to back would last about five years and five months, the first month is for the Temporary Order and the Request for a Hearing. That's why it's impossible to have served five different Restraining Orders on one person and keep those Restraining Orders in force in less than four years.

No normal person would stay married to anyone for four years and keep serving Restraining Order after Restraining Order on another person to begin with. It would be easier to file a divorce and have a Stipulated Divorce Decree not allowing any contact and Totally Restraining someone from coming around you or contacting you, that way you don't have to keep going back to court. I don't know why some judge didn't catch that fact, it doesn't take a rocket scientist to realize what Brenda was doing. Every judge Brenda had sign one of those five Restraining Orders and the Orders to drop the Restraining Orders was in the Umatilla County Courthouse in Pendleton, Oregon. Anyway, Brenda dropped the Restraining Order and I moved back in with her and Stevey, we still lived in the same townhouse she fell down the stairs in when I was gone.

After Jeff was born, the judge ordered a Dismissal of the Divorce Proceedings because of the Want of Prosecution on December 21, 1989 (Evidence Section Page 12.), in other words, Brenda never filed the Final Divorce Order, so the judge couldn't sign it, the judge finally dropped the case because no action was ever taken in the case. Brenda never really wanted the divorce or the Restraining Order to begin with, they were just a way to keep control of me. Of course during this time Brenda called Jesse and told Jesse that Brenda had put a Restraining Order on me even though the Restraining Order was on me for less than a week. Brenda found out she could use that leverage to keep control.

A few years went by and we went to Marriage Counseling through the Umatilla County Mental Health in Pendleton, Oregon. During this time, we were seeing Jacob, even though Jesse didn't like it. Eventually Jesse found an attorney that took it all back to court for no reason. You'll see what I mean. So we had to find an attorney as well. When you go to the court system, no one wins but the attorneys and if you don't have the money, they don't want anything to do with you. That should tell everyone something about who, or what, I should say, they really care about. They don't care about the children involved, they don't care about the families who suffer, all they care about is their money.

Jesse finally decides to take me to court again (Evidence Section 13-20.). We get to court on April 8, 1992 and the judge modifies the decree. We no sooner get the Modified Decree back and Jesse has her attorney write another letter dated May 26, 1992 (Evidence Section Page 21.). I am going to type in part of what Jesse's attorney wrote because I am not sure you can read it.

The area of the Evidence Section that was black highlighted on Page 21 reads, "Brenda indicated to Jesse that she and Walter Burchett are currently separated and that she had some concerns regarding his exercise of visitation with Jesse and Walter's child Jacob. The upshot of that conversation was that Brenda turned Walter into Children's Services Division for abuse sometime in March 1992, that one of the reasons for the separation in their marriage was his temper and tendencies toward violent behavior. Brenda and Jesse worked out an agreement whereby the visitation on May 17, 1992 could take place, but that Brenda would closely monitor that visitation, and in fact, Jacob would be staying with Brenda."

Now what's wrong with these statements? Well, first of all it was never up to Jesse, Brenda or any attorney to stipulate any visitation without first going through the proper legal channels, which no one did. Second, having concerns is not a legal reason for taking the law into your own hands, especially when there is an Order already signed by the judge allowing Unsupervised Visitation. That Unsupervised Visitation Order doesn't state that anyone needs to be with me, that's why it's called, Unsupervised

Visitation in the first place. "This was agreeable to Jesse as she is desirous of having Jacob get to know his Siblings." Third, it doesn't matter whether it's agreeable to Jesse or not, the judge signed the Order and there was no reason for the visitation not to take place, Jesse isn't a judge, nor is any attorney. It is desirable for the custodial parent to be agreeable to things, but not mandatory. "Apparently, Walter was not enthusiastic about this arrangement and made several threats to Brenda regarding her children as well as Jacob." Fourth, at no time did Jesse or any attorney ever hear me make any threats to Brenda, Stevey, Jeff, or Paul, because I never did make any threats toward any of them. Jesse just didn't want me to see Jacob and Brenda was ticked off at me because she didn't have control over anything.

The one part of this letter that is true is that I was not enthusiastic about the arrangement. When two or more women get together and scheme, they may get their way in the short term, but everyone looses in the long-term, except the attorneys. I didn't agree with the arrangement because that's not what the Order said. It's time custodial parents realize that when a judge orders something, that's exactly what the judge means, not that you can walk right out of the court room and do whatever you want. "I want to inform you by this letter, that I have advised my client that unless and until we can work something out where we can be assured that Jacob will not be in a precarious situation, that the summer visitation should not take place as planned."

On June 9, 1992 Brenda writes a letter to Jesse's attorney (Evidence Section Page 23-25.). Now that Brenda and I are back together again, Brenda sees a chance to take control of the situation and be in charge. If you notice, when Brenda and I are fighting she has no one else to fight with. It's the times Brenda and I are fighting and not around each other or legally separated, that she sides with Jesse. Brenda's gratification is Jesse giving Brenda control which feeds Brenda's self-image. Anyway, Brenda writes, 'Somewhere between what I said to Jesse and what Jesse said to you, and what you wrote down, the information has been twisted around.' Did Brenda actually say all those things when she was separated from me or not? I don't know, I wasn't there. Brenda continues, 'I would like to take this opportunity to clear a few things up before another two years to go by before we get Jacob again, I really don't want to go back to court.' Brenda did try to clear things up, but only after we were back together again, which didn't do any good. Once something is said that's going to help an attorney win their case, the attorney isn't interested in hearing anything else. You see, when Brenda was in between sides, she could say anything she wanted and get away with it because there was no one to confirm or deny whatever she said. Once she was on my side or Jesse's side, Brenda had to stick with whatever she said for that particular side.

The second paragraph, 'One thing you got wrong in your letter was the misinformation of me (Brenda) turning Walter into CSD. for abuse. The facts are, as of March 1992 Mental Health, Stevey's therapist, turned Walter into CSD to explain the mark. I will tell you what actually happened, the therapist asked me about the mark on Stevey's face. I said his dad slapped him a crossed the face the day before. The therapist viewed this as abuse and called CSD.' This is true, Brenda didn't turn me into Children Services Division for abuse. The Mental Health Therapist actually gave me the phone in his office, then he dialed the number and I talked to Children Services Division myself.

Therapists always sees things as abuse until they are told it's not, then they agree with someone else. They're a bunch of chickens when it comes to making decisions. Therapists always waits for someone else in a different department or higher up to make a decision and then always agrees with someone else's decision. 'When I talked to our case worker, she agreed this was the case and it was not abuse, so they entered us (both Walt and I) in a Behavioral Management program.' This is true, and of course the Mental Health Therapist who originally viewed the red mark as abuse quickly changed his mind and sided with CSD, that it was just me not knowing my own strength and not abuse. Mental Health Therapists don't know what is and isn't abuse, but are afraid to admit it, yet they are the ones who are supposed to be the authority on abuse since they are the counselors. To be totally honest here, not even Children's Services Division can call anything 'abuse'. All anyone can do is describe the symptoms and details, it actually takes a judge to decide if something is abuse or not. 'This program gives us new ways to discipline the children, and teaches us to learn when we need a time out.' This is true; however, nothing will ever take the place of a good old fashioned spanking from time to time. That's why Jesus recommends that parents spank their children to keep them in line, but only using as much force as necessary to do the intended job. 'We both have been going faithfully to this program for over a month and a half.' That is true. 'This program should prove to you that Walt is learning new techniques to discipline children. I can honestly say that he is changing and growing.' Now look at that statement again will you? Brenda is saying that I am changing and growing, then why is it that when we are separated that she always says I'm 'unfit'? Because she knows that if she tells the truth that she will loose the children. Also notice that Brenda says nothing about her growth or honesty in different situations here, maybe that's because she didn't grow or change in any way. 'He takes the kids situations now with patience and understanding and not quick to react with discipline.' To be real honest with everyone, I always did do this. 'He gets the facts first and then disciplines, but not with physical punishment.' This depends on the age of the child and what they did wrong, at that time, I didn't need to physically punish them unless they said a swear word like Stevey did when I slapped him. Why didn't Brenda and I use soap and water? Actually we tried that approach first and it didn't work. Sure Stevey stuck out his tongue and we put a drop of liquid soap on his tongue, but a couple of days later, he slipped with another swear word. 'He now stands them in the corner, or makes him sit in a time-out chair, or takes privileges away from him.' This is true, I did give these things a try.

'The second thing wrong is during the weekend of May 17, 1992 Walt and I agreed to live together that weekend before I even talked to Jesse.' This is true, Brenda and I did sit down and discuss all the living arrangements before all this happened. You need to understand something. It had been years since Jacob and I even was able to see each other and I really wanted to spend some quality time with Jacob. One-on-one time for us to get to know each other without having Stevey or Brenda around, doing things as a family is good, but a parent needs time alone with each child as well. 'What I said was he would not go for living with me the whole time Jacob is down here for the summer.' That is true, as I just said, I wanted some one-on-one time with Jacob. 'He did not make several threats to me because we had already agreed to live together that weekend.' This is true as well.

'The situation in which I dropped Walt off in Madras while I continued on to Bend was not because Walt was loosing his temper with the children, but because he was nervous about going to Bend.' This is true, to this day, I don't like being around either Jesse or Brenda, nor do I like talking to either of them. They can never make up what they took from me, I don't trust either one of them. 'I told Jesse I dropped him off in Madras because his nerves were on edge and I wanted him to be able to settle down.' This is what Brenda told me when she returned to Madras where I was waiting for her. 'Walt gets nervous every time he goes to Bend because of having to see Jesse.' This is true, anytime I see or hear from Jesse I get very nervous, and I am that way with Brenda now as well, if you had all this happen to you, you would be very nervous too. 'Besides, do you actually think I would drop Walt off in Madras with a 3 month old baby if I thought his temper was out of control?' This is true, Paul did stay behind with me that day for several hours while Brenda and the other boys continued down to Bend, Oregon to pick Jeff up. Paul mostly slept, but there were a few times I had to feed him and burp him. 'The answer is no! Yes, I dropped Walt off with a 3 month old baby (Paul) in Madras while I continued to Bend with the other three kids because of Walt's nerves not his temper.' This is true. 'If his temper was out of control, I would not have trusted him with the care of a three month old baby. Kelly, our attorney's legal assistant, told us Walt could be dropped off anywhere, anytime he wanted because he doesn't even need to go.' This is true, the Modification of Decree did not say I had to pick Jacob up or drop him off, just that I had Unsupervised Visitations with Jacob, I could send anyone down to Bend, Oregon and pick up and drop Jacob off. Jesse did ask me that if I did send someone else down that the person be someone Jacob was acquainted with and I knew Jesse was right about that and did that even though it wasn't written in the Order. I didn't even have to have anyone around me during the whole time Jacob and I were together. 'When I got back to Madras, Walt and the baby were just fine.' This is true.

'I would like to take this opportunity to tell you a few things. First, I can understand why Jesse is concerned while Jacob is down here. She would not be a normal mother if she wasn't, but there is a time you have to open yourself up and learn to trust again. As Jesse and I talked and compared the past abuse on both of us, we sort of established a bond and agreed was off the record and would be kept between the two of us.' You notice both Brenda and Jesse are using each other to get what each of them want? Jesse not knowing anything other than what Brenda tells her and Brenda always wanting to be in control and changing her story all the time. If you also notice Brenda never said the past abuse on both of them was from me, just the past abuse on both of them. Brenda had prior abuse and had been raped before I ever met her and Jesse was accosted by some distant relative while her family went out somewhere when she was a little girl. Jesse only told me about it once and I never pried, so I really can't remember much about that. As I sit here typing on this computer, I wonder if that was one of the things Jesse shared with Brenda that day. 'However, since it seems that this is where it is not going to stay, I will be just as open and honest with you as I have been with Jesse. Second, there were times I was afraid of Walter, but like I told Jesse the abuse that has gone on in the past in my relationship has taken the both of us to cause and it has not been directed towards the kids.' Brenda is honest about that, the biggest problem Brenda has is, she needs to be in control. According to the Word of God, the man has to be the head of the house, the more I tried to be the head of the house the more Brenda fought me in that aspect. 'See, I have a mouth on me that can say hurtful things without realizing I say them,' Brenda admits here that she still has a mouth on her that hurts people and that is 'mental abuse'. 'Walt used to have an exploding temper.' Notice Brenda, herself says I used to have, hey, that's past tense (Actually I just put my foot down and that's what she didn't like. No exploding temper, just told her this is the way it has to be, period. She didn't like it so she rebelled.). 'These are the reasons we are separated, but we are in marriage counseling and we have been in it for a month and a half. Walt's learned ways to control his temper', everyone has a temper to one degree or another, if you don't believe that then you think you are better than Jesus Himself. Jesus has a temper and we are created in the image of God. The big thing is to learn how much of that temper you need to use and when. 'And I've learned ways to control my mouth,- to think before I speak.' I wish she would have, but she never. I even heard through the grape vine Brenda used her tongue against one of the teachers in the Umatilla School District in Umatilla, Oregon a few years back. From what I understand, Brenda is always threatening a law suit against the teachers in the Umatilla School District.

     'I know one of the questions you have, is do I trust Walt alone with the children. I will explain this to you with a few situations. One day, I went to Salem overnight and left him alone with all the our kids.' This is true, she did leave me with all the children. At the time we were going to the Salvation Army Church in Pendleton, Oregon where the Captain and his wife were in charge of the mission outlet. In fact, we had the boys dedicated on their 'Cradle Roll'. The Salvation Army was having a get together for all the women of the churches and there was a women's group in the Pendleton Branch who went down to Salem. 'These kids are not ordinary by any means either. One, the oldest, has an Attention Deficit Hyperactive Disorder, the middle child is a disabled child who only communicates by screaming, and the last is a baby. These kids can get on anybody's nerves,' actually all this really didn't bother me. With Stevey, I put him to work being my helper with the other two and Stevey liked being daddy's helper. With Jeff, I just told him to settle down and speak slower, he did and I could understand what he was saying. Jeff was just getting to be able to talk, not too well, but talk. Paul was asleep most of the time, so taking care of the three boys was really fun. 'but I left him alone with them overnight and he was fine.' Actually, I wish Brenda would have stayed gone longer than she did, the boys and I were having fun and enjoying ourselves. 'The kids were all in tact when I got home.' This is true, of course they were all ok, that was one of the few times we all had a great time together, Brenda wasn't around to bother us, Brenda went to her women's meeting, me and the boys had our own men's night out away from Brenda, it was great. 'There were times on the whole trip to Salem I wanted to call home to check up on him,' This is true, according to the Captain's wife, the women dropped Brenda off and the Captain's wife did tell me Brenda wanted to call home to see if everything was ok, but the women in the group kept telling Brenda, trust Walter, he knows what he is doing, the boys will be ok., the boy's were just fine when the women got back and dropped Brenda off. 'but I didn't because I wanted to show him

I trusted him. This overnight trip was after March 1992, it was the last of April 1992', this is true. (During the time we attended the Salvation Army, I told the Captain of the beatings I was getting from Brenda. He did put me up in a motel room for a weekend to see if that would help, but two hours after I checked in Brenda put the boys in the car and drove to each motel until she found my car, that didn't do any good. Pendleton, Oregon is too small to try to hide in a motel room.)

'I also leave him alone with the kids every Thursday night for a few hours, so I can have time away.' This is true, Brenda went to the Ladies Auxiliary at the Salvation Army Church every Thursday night. 'The point I'm trying to make is, we all make mistakes and have in our past, but we learn from those mistakes. Walt is learning from his mistakes and so am I. We have sought help-professional and are trying to put our lives back together again. We have even sought help in the disciplining our children so we can agree on the discipline without physical punishment.' This is true, we did go to marriage counseling several times, but every time she would revert back to her old ways. My honest opinion is that she has a deeper problem than what marriage counseling would ever be able to resolve. I wonder if her brother raping her all those years made her where, if she couldn't keep control, she would fight back to regain control because she couldn't control her brother raping her. He did give her a choice, he would either have sex with Brenda or he would take either June, Brenda's younger sister, or Barbara, Brenda's older sister. Brenda did control that part, but the actual molestation she didn't have any control over.

'Jacob came back this last time unharmed, not because I closely supervised,' Brenda admits that she didn't supervise anything. 'but because Walt and I are learning new discipline techniques. I can assure you that Jacob will always come back unharmed.' Brenda admits there is nothing wrong with the way I take care of the boys. 'As far as the summer goes, Jacob will live with me part of the time and will be with Walt part of the time.' Brenda admits our living arrangements will be separate and is already set up. We will separately have all the boys part of the time. 'Some of the time Jacob will be with the both of us together.' This is true. 'And all of the time Jacob will be with his brothers.' This is true, that's the way it was set up. Wherever Jacob goes, his brothers will go and wherever his brothers go, Jacob will go. I think we deserve this summer with our son. We have given you no reason to think otherwise.' To be totally honest, it's really none of Jesse's business, even as a custodial parent where Jacob is as long as he is fine and back on time. On June 19, 1992 Brenda wrote things down on a piece of paper that Jacob told us both at our dining room table once. I'm not going to add any comments to those statements, how can I? (Evidence Section Page 26-27.).

There were certain days and times Jacob was supposed to call Jesse in Bend, whether he was with me or Brenda. When Jacob was with me and Brenda I made sure Jacob made the calls to Jesse at that particular time. After that, my visitation time with Jacob, Jeff, and Stevey started. Every time Jacob was to make the call to Jesse, I made sure we went over to a pay phone and made the call. Brenda just couldn't help but come around, you see, Brenda and I weren't really living together, but we weren't legally separated either. Brenda came over with Paul and one time in particular my sister, Linda, Joe, (Linda's husband) Susie, Jamie, and Tabitha (Linda's daughters) showed up at the same time, Joe, Linda and the girls were planning a family outing and they were all going swimming. They invited Brenda, Jacob, Jeff, and Stevey to go with them. It would be a few hours break for me, which I really didn't need, but if Linda, and Joe wanted to take Brenda and the boys with them so all the kids could have fun together, I couldn't see anything wrong with it, so I said, 'Ok, as long as Jacob gets to make the call to Jesse I don't care.' They were going to Plymouth Beach, that is on the Washington Side of the Columbia River, right across from Umatilla, Oregon. There was a family picnic area and swimming there. The water from the Columbia River goes into an inlet and becomes very slow, there are no undertows and no swift current in there, the water also goes through an outlet so the water isn't stale either. See, the Columbia River is known World Wide to be a very dangerous river. Well, that is a very true statement, the Columbia River is no river to mess around with. There are a lot of undertows in it, especially right below the dams. The family outing was right below McNary Dam in Plymouth, Washington, but totally safe from all the undertows, it has a very low water speed in there just like any other swimming hole. There is also a swimming area right above the McNary Dam in Umatilla, Oregon that is safe to swim in. Anyway, Brenda drives in earlier than I expected, while she was dropping the boys off I asked her if Jacob had made his phone call. Brenda didn't answer me and heads out. I could tell she was upset about something, but didn't know what, and she wouldn't talk to me for some reason. Shortly after Brenda leaves, Joe and Linda drive in with the girls. I asked them if Jacob had made his call to Bend like he was supposed to and they told me there were no phones in the area to call, so Jacob couldn't make the call. Brenda was supposed to see that Jacob made the call to Jesse down in Bend, Oregon at the specified time that evening because Jacob wasn't with me that evening to make the call, he was with Brenda. Joe told me Brenda got upset because Stevey was floating on one of those inflatable rafts and the raft drifted a little deeper than Brenda thought was safe. Brenda waded out to get Stevey, but couldn't because she was too short, so Joe waded out and got Stevey. Apparently everyone started talking and forgot about Stevey floating on the inflatable raft.

Brenda got angry and called Jesse and told Jesse that Brenda saw the boys in the same clothes for three days. Well, Brenda did see the boys in the same clothes for three days. The reason was that every time Jacob came down, Jesse would go through all his clothes upon returning to Bend just to make sure we didn't miss anything, and if we forgot something I would get in trouble, so instead of making the boys change, I waited until they had their baths each night and took their clothes and washed their clothes in mom's washer and dryer each night so the clothes were always clean the next morning. At times it was hard to keep Jacob in his clothes. You need to know, Stanfield, Oregon is in the desert and in the summer time, it's not uncommon for temperatures to reach one hundred and one degrees or higher. Jacob was coming right into a heat wave from Bend, Oregon a nice cool mountainous area where Mount Bachelor and the Three Sisters are. Mount Bachelor and the Three Sisters are famous for skiing slopes. So yes, Jacob was hot when he came up for visitation. To this day, I remember putting their clothes on them several times during the day just for them to take their clothes off again within a five minute time span. Most of the time it wasn't even five minutes, they would just run out of my reach and there clothes would come off again. It was just too hot, and with them being little boys, no one complained because even the adults wished they could shed some clothes during the fourth of July week. The Stanfield Police even drove by a couple of times and never said a word about how the boys were dressed, or in this case I should say, undressed. Anyway, Brenda just can't leave things alone without being in charge so she calls Jesse, Jesse and her parents come up from Bend.

I usually did some kind of repair work on mom's house while I was staying there, but that week I didn't even pick up a wrench or a screwdriver. I didn't want anything to happen that would give anyone any reason to think I wasn't taking care of the boys right, so I didn't do any work during that week at all. I pretty much sat on the steps or was sitting in a chair on the side of mom's house watching the boys play all day, every day. The next day Jesse drives up at mom's and the boys and I are outside, it wasn't like Jesse to come all the way up to Stanfield from Bend just to talk to me. Jesse and I talk for a few minutes about Jacob not calling the night before. I told Jesse that Jacob was with Brenda and Joe told me there were no phones in the area. I thought Jesse was satisfied with the explanation and since there were three adults with Jacob that everything was alright, all of a sudden Brenda drives up at the house too well, now I'm really wondering what's going on. All three of us are talking and Jesse and Brenda decide between the two of them, if I wanted to take Paul along with Jacob, Stevey, and Jeff that Jesse and Brenda can go Yard Sale Shopping together. I didn't care, so I said sure, I'll take all four of the boys. So Jesse and Brenda went Yard Sale Shopping. Well, in Stanfield, there aren't that many Yard Sales to shop in, even during the summer months. There was a four family Yard Sale that was a decent size, but the other two were very small. I saw the yard sales when I went to get mom's mail at the Stanfield Post Office. Jesse and Brenda were gone for four hours. Yes, I remember it quite well, I looked at my watch and knowing there were only three yard sales in town that wouldn't take four hours, not even for women. I just knew in my heart something else was going on, I didn't care about Jesse and Brenda being gone that long. I would rather have had them tell me the truth and say, 'We'll be gone all afternoon because of such and such', than to lie to me. Jesse and Brenda couldn't have told me the truth though as you will read a little later. Jesse and Brenda had to keep what they were really up to a secret from me, they were already scheming for something more drastic than any yard sale. Anyway, I watched Jacob, Stevey, Jeff, and Paul for four full hours, which was actually fun to do. With the other three boys there, they were helping dad watch their little brother. Jacob, Stevey, and Jeff all enjoyed helping me watch Paul. What was Paul doing? Paul was doing what all infants do, he was sleeping, playing with his little hand toys, teething, eating (sucking on his bottle), and burping. Jacob, Stevey, and Jeff actually took turns giving Paul his toy when he dropped it. Jacob, Stevey, and Jeff wouldn't leave Paul's side when he was awake because they were afraid they would miss their turn in giving his toy back to him. Then it came to Paul being hungry. Well, as long as Paul was in his little carrier, Jacob and Stevey were old enough to help me, I supervised, but Jeff just wasn't big enough to do much. Jacob and Stevey held the bottle up for Paul while he was sucking on the nipple. I told Jacob to watch us and make sure we do everything like we are supposed to. I showed Jacob and Stevey how to hold the bottle to Paul's mouth, the angle, the formula level, all that stuff and then I looked over at Jeff and asked, 'Right Jeff?' Jeff agreed with me, but it also made Jeff feel included in what I was doing so he didn't feel left out. So Jeff supervised Jacob and Stevey helping me feed Paul. When it came to burping Paul, Jacob and Stevey both wanted to, but I just didn't feel right with the way they were trying to hold Paul, so I told them to go play again and I did the burping and walking with Paul when he had to burp and to put him to sleep again. Well, Jesse and Brenda made it back and told me they also went up to Pendleton to our house.

On July 8, 1992 mom sent me to Bi-Mart in Pendleton, Oregon to buy some car ramps and I took Jacob with me. Jeff and Stevey stayed with mom during those two hours. It felt good just to have Jacob with me one-on-one for a while. When Jacob and I got to Bi-Mart I saw a popcorn stand, so I bought a bag of popcorn for Jacob and I to share while we walked around a little. When Jacob and I finished the popcorn (I let Jacob have most of the popcorn. It wasn't the popcorn I wanted as much as it was the time with Jacob and the two of us sharing that I was after.) we found the car ramps and bought them for mom. The time I had with Jacob was so good, it felt like it was too good to be true. Well, it was too good to be true, during the time Jacob and I were sharing our popcorn together, Jesse had met Brenda and Jesse and Brenda went to mom's to pick up the boys and their things. Brenda sent Stevey into mom's house to get all the boy's clothes. Mom was laying down on the couch to take a nap and heard Stevey come in, but didn't worry about it because during that week the boys were always going in and out. When mom was home during the summer, she always kept her doors open just in case a little breeze came up, the breeze would go into her house and cool it off a little, she didn't own an air conditioner back then.

When Jacob and I returned from Pendleton, Oregon back to mom's, we no sooner got into the yard and was in the process of unloading the car ramps than I see Jesse at the gate of mom's chain link fence and Darla, Jesse's mother calling for Jacob to come to her. All this is in the Stanfield Police Report made out by the Corporal of the Stanfield Police Department (Evidence Section Page 28-32.). Under 'Action Taken', you notice 'He told me that Jesse had called Jacob over to her parents car to talk to him. She would not tell him why she wanted to talk to him, so he restrained Jacob from going. (Now remember, I had an Order signed by the judge for those particular days and this particular day was one of the days on that list. Yes, I wanted to know why, wouldn't any parent?) Rick, Darla, and Jesse got out of the vehicle and walked over onto his yard in front of the residence. Rick grabbed Walter in a bear hug to restrain him. (That is true, Rick did put me in a bear hug and I was concentrating more on Jacob's safety and welfare than anything else. I knew something was going to happen and didn't want Jacob to get hurt in the process.) Walter said that Rick punched him on the left jaw area of his face during the fight causing discomfort. But no outward sign of injury or swelling. (This is true, and right now I'd like to mention that if a grown man can punch me in the jaw area without showing any signs of injury or swelling, just think about what a woman could do to a man without showing any signs of battery.) His ex-wife removed Jacob and took him with her parents from the residence yard area. (Even being a custodial parent doesn't give anyone the legal right to go onto someone's private property to retrieve any child.) They had left just prior to my arrival at 12:30. Brenda removed three children from the residence also, but Walt was not concerned about this. (I wasn't concerned about it at the time because I didn't know Brenda even had a part in the plot to take the boys. Walt's mother, told me that she heard a commotion outside of her residence in the yard. (Mom was still on the couch laying down.) She observed Walter and Rick fighting in the front yard. (Mom finally got to the front door.) I contacted Brenda at her parents home located at 26 Pomono Drive in Umatilla, Oregon. She told me that Jesse and her were concerned about the children's welfare at Walt's residence. She said that they contacted Julie at the CSD (Children's Services Division) Office in Pendleton, Oregon asking for help in removing the children due to neglect. Julie and the State Police adjacent to Children's Services Division in Pendleton declined to help them. (Now see? They went to Children's Services Division and the State Police and not even Children's Services Division had any reason to remove the boys from my care. Is a custodial parent more powerful than Children Services? Apparently they are.) Jesse and her did not attempt to contact the Stanfield Police Department to help with a complaint. They also did not contact the local Children's Services Division Office in Hermiston, Oregon for assistance. They decided between them that they would remove the children without Children's Services Division intervention. (Now that's clearly taking the law into your own hands and against the law.) Brenda told me that the children had been left in the same clothing for approximately 3 days. The children were allowed to wear their shoes with no socks or go bare feet. They had developed sores on their feet. (And no one asked me anything about any of this.) I did not observe the children's feet. She told me that the Perpetrators were in route back to Bend, Oregon. (Later I found out it was Brenda's dad who gave Rick, Darla, and Jesse the idea to go over the Columbia River on the Washington Side and down the highway there, then cross back over the Columbia River at Biggs, Oregon to head down to Bend, Oregon. Brenda's dad helped with all this and I didn't know anything about any of it at that time. The Oregon State Police were looking for Rick, Darla, Jesse, and Jacob on the Oregon Side, not the Washington Side. The Umatilla County District Attorney was going to have the Oregon State Police return Jacob to me because the dates were clearly written out in the Revised Divorce Decree.) She did not know where they lived, but gave me Jesse's Attorney's name.' Now skip two paragraphs and go to, 'On July,….The boy was neglected and was not allowed to call his mother as set out in the Custody Decree. Darla told me that she had tried to call Jacob away from Walter in the front yard area of the residence and Walter had grabbed her across the fence at the edge of the yard to keep her from taking to Jacob. She told me that her husband Rick, had gotten out of their car to help her and during a struggle with Walt and had been hit. (Rick, I did pull back to hit you, but someone yelled, 'don't hit him, he's got a heart condition', so I didn't hit you. If I would have hit you, you would have been hitting your butt on the sidewalk. Later I found out it was Brenda who yelled that.) She said that Walt had bruised her arm also. Her husband is 98 percent disabled from a saw mill accident. He has one shoulder fused at the socket and is unable to move much more than a clamping type motion with his arms. He may be able to punch someone with a blow delivered with a reduced force. She told me that her daughter's attorney in Bend had instructed her to remove Jacob from Walter's care. (I didn't know any attorney was wearing a black robe now. Apparently attorney's have more power than an Order signed by a judge.) On July 17, 1992, at 1043 hrs., I was able to phone Rick in Bend, Oregon. Rick told me that he got out of his car when Walter was attempting to restrain Jacob from going with his mother and grandmother. He contained Walt in a Bear hug and was punched in the chest by Walter. He returned a punch to Walter and then left the scene. He was advised that a report would be forwarded to the Umatilla County District Attorney for possible assault charges and Possible Custodial Interference charges. (Nothing ever came from any of this. They get away with kidnapping and nothing happens. I kind of wonder if this incident right here is why Brenda and her boyfriend at that time kidnapped the boys from the Foster Care and took the boys over the Oregon/California State Line as well. Brenda saw Jesse get away with it, so Brenda did it with her boyfriend and they got away with it as well, at least so far they have. There isn't any Statute of Limitation for Kidnapping three minor children out of Foster Care and the boys being the Ward of the Court at that time. I wonder why the Federal Bureau of Investigation wasn't called in on this.)

You notice Brenda runs to the Court House and fills out a Petition for a Temporary Restraining Order on July 9, 1992 and Temporary Restraining Order was issued on July 10, 1992 (Evidence Section Page 33-40.). If she was that concerned about the boys, she could have filled out a Petition and had an Order done before Jesse even came up from Bend, OR. No mother in her right mind, when they think their child is really in danger is going to wait and leave the children in the person's care they are supposed to be afraid of in the first place. Of course the day after the Petition is filed, the Temporary Restraining Order is granted, and then I asked for a hearing and Brenda drops the Restraining Order before the hearing date even comes around. It sure looks good on paper in front of a judge for the woman if she ever wants to divorce a man and keep the children, doesn't it. Judges never do hear any evidence on why the Temporary Restraining Orders are filed in the first place, all they see is that one has been filed and later dropped, if the report is even brought to their attention. Nice work women, you've manipulated the court system and the judges have allowed it. Of course, I go up and filed a Temporary Restraining Order that later became a Restraining Order for one year on Jesse, but it really didn't do any good (Evidence Section Page 41-44.). You see, a Restraining Order is only good within that particular county and since Jesse lived in Deschutes County, in Bend, Oregon at the time, the Umatilla County Restraining Order never did anything and by the time the Restraining Order was to die Jesse and I would have been in court again anyway for the Revision of the Revised Dissolution of Marriage and Visitation Rights Hearing, but I couldn't afford an attorney and Jesse knew it. I heard that Jesse and her attorney actually laughed about the Restraining Order I served on Jesse. Jesse got who she came for and that's all she wanted. She got away with it too, or so it seems so far. Like I said, Kidnapping has no Statue of Limitations and they took Jacob over a state line twice, once going over the Columbia River and once coming back across the Columbia River. The day they took Jacob was actually in the Decree as the actual date, July 8, 1992, the dates were in black and white. I was to have Jacob until July 12, 1992 I believe it was. Brenda came back about a week and a half later wanting to make up. Like I said, the Respondent is not allowed to contact the Petitioner, remember? I went back for the kids sake, I missed Jacob growing up so far and didn't want to miss Jeff and Paul growing up as well.

On July 22, 1992 Jesse went to her attorney's office and made out the Affidavit in Support of Motion to Show Cause. The Sixth Paragraph states (Evidence Section Page 45-47.): 'During the second modification proceeding, I was willing to further expand that visitation as well as establish specific visitation for two primary reasons. (First of all Jesse, it wasn't up to you to expand anything, the judge did the expanding in the order he signed. Those orders are still in effect even though we were talking through attorneys.) Respondent had remarried and I had come to feel that his current wife Brenda, was a very responsible woman, who was capable of looking out for the safety of our son Jacob. (Read on Jesse, you'll find out how responsible Brenda really is, or should I say, irresponsible.) Secondly, our son is now eight years old, and I felt that it was very important for him to get to know his father. (Not important enough to listen to the proper authorities though, huh? If I had done what Jesse and Brenda did, I'd have been locked up for it and the authorities would have thrown the key away, that's the difference between being a man and a woman, a man can't do anything, but a woman can get away with almost everything.)

After entering into the second modification in April 1992, I came to find out directly from Respondent's current wife, Brenda, that they had separated and that he had left the family home. She further indicated to me that one of the primary reasons that she had separated from Respondent was because of his abusive behavior towards both her and their children. (Now this is a counter-diction of statements. The sentence right before this one says 'he had left the family home', that's an indication that I left her, not that she left me. In other words, I had separated from Brenda, but I did want time with my boys alone, without anyone, but my mom around. Even that was too much to ask. To this day, my mother is afraid of Brenda and she is 76 years old, my mom has been through a lot and to have my mom afraid of Brenda says a lot about how bad Brenda really is.) As a result of this, I had some concerns and discussed these concerns with my attorney. She in turn, expressed those concerns to Respondent, through a letter to his attorney, at the time. That letter resulted in further exchange in communication, with the end result being that I allowed our son Jacob to go for the first segment of the scheduled summer visitation because of a representation by Respondent, and confirmed by a letter from his therapist, that he was in counseling on many issues including parenting. I would not have allowed Jacob to go for that summer visitation without Respondent being in counseling. (It's not for you to decide, when a judge signs an Order, that Order is to be followed unless the proper authorities intervene, and in this case they found no reason to intervene.) Additionally, I was advised by Respondent's current wife that Jacob would be spending much of his time with his brothers, in her home. (It doesn't matter where the child spends his time with the non-custodial parent as long as it's not immoral or illegal. That's the non-custodial parents time with the child.) This arrangement made me more comfortable because I felt that she would look out for his safety as well as the fact that Jacob would get an opportunity to get to know his brothers.

On July 8, 1992, towards the end of the first segment of Respondent's summer visitation with our son, I received a fairly frantic telephone call from Brenda. (That's because she wasn't in control anymore and had to be in the 'spot light'.) She indicated to me that Jacob had spend most of the first couple of weeks at her place, with Respondent visiting him there. However, she indicated that Respondent had taken her children and Jacob to Respondent's mother's home in Stanfield, Oregon on approximately July 5, 1992 (Just like we all agreed.).

Brenda indicated to me that she had gone to visit the children on July 8, 1992, found them to be in the same clothes that they were in when she sent them with the Respondent on July 5, (That's because I kept washing them every night because Jesse kept having a cow if I forget to put some little thing back in the suitcase.) and further witnessed abusive behavior by Respondent against her children (Now Brenda is making things up. That's the only way she could get attention on her again. She was taken out of the 'spot light' and had to have attention again. If this was really true then Children Services and the State Police would have helped them pick the boys up in the first place, but as you have read, Children Services and the State Police refused to do anything because nothing was wrong.) and witnessed respondent pulling and jerking our son Jacob by the arm. (This is not true.) at times the boys were filthy, (They were playing hard in the yard, the yard has dirt, of course they were dirty. I didn't keep them in the house all day long like Jesse and Brenda did. I let the boys play hard outside in mom's yard with a chain link fence around it. They were totally safe.) she also observed that Jacob had blisters and sores all over his feet. (As I said before, if Jacob had blisters, Jesse would have seen them when Jesse and Brenda met before going to Children Services Division and the Oregon State Police for four hours that day leaving all four boys in my care, remember? There were no blisters on Jacob's feet or Jesse would have told CSD and would have picked Jacob up right then.) Brenda tried to take all of the children from the home, however, Respondent indicated to her that she could remove her two children, but would not be allowed to take Jacob. (I reminded Brenda that this was my time with the boys and asked her why she wanted the boys anyway, she was supposed to be having a break from them in the first place.) Not wanting Jacob to be by himself with Respondent, Brenda allowed all three children to remain there and returned to her home. (Now what father or mother is going to do this if they have a legal choice? Leaving their own child in danger? If there really was any danger, Brenda would have called for help.) She then called me because as she indicated to me, she was extremely concerned about Jacob's welfare and about Respondent's increasing violent temper. (If Brenda was really so concerned about all this, then why did she keep coming back to me and keep dropping Restraining Order after Restraining Order? She wasn't concerned, she thrived on being in control.) Brenda also indicated that Jacob and his step-brother, Stevey, had tried to run away during the visit, rather than go to Respondent's. (That's not true at all. What happened was they started talking about a few toys that Jacob had at home and they wanted to play with those toys for a while. So they decided they were going to Bend, Oregon to play with Jacob's toys, then come back home, to Pendleton, Oregon in a couple of hours. They couldn't understand the mileage between Bend, Oregon and Pendleton, Oregon was 250 miles one way, they always went to sleep all the way over and back. As far as they knew it wouldn't take over a couple of minutes to walk to Jacob's and a couple of minutes to walk back. That's why they decided to go to Jacob's home, play with the toys for a few hours and come back home. This one isn't even in the papers, but I'll tell you anyway. Brenda and I were downstairs in our townhouse. Jacob and Stevey were upstairs playing in Stevey's room. It seemed really quiet for a long time so I decided I better check on them to see if everything was ok. I opened the door to Stevey's bedroom and there they were, both with their knees on the carpet floor sitting, patiently watching a bed lamp that they had turned on and had accidentally fallen to the floor while they were playing. I asked them what they were doing and they both said, they were waiting for the lamp to start a fire. We know that a lamp that is left on can start a fire, and if there is a fire then we are supposed to go for help, so we are waiting for a fire to start so we can get help. I asked them, Why they didn't just pick the lamp up and turn the light off before the fire starts? Jacob said they aren't supposed to touch anything that is plugged into the wall because we might get shocked, so they had to wait for the lamp to start a fire to get help. Honest to God, they were sitting there with their eyes glued to that burning light bulb just waiting for that fire to start so they could come to us for help. The bulb actually did burn a hole in the carpet and ruined the lamp shade, the Good Lord just told me I needed to go check on them because there was something wrong. Brenda told Jesse what happened when we dropped Jacob off and Jesse asked Brenda what I did. Brenda told Jesse I handled the situation very well, he explained to them both it was ok to turn the lamp off and actually had both of them turn the lamp on and off while he was watching them, so they would know they were allowed to turn the lamp on and off even if it was plugged into the wall and then he took a walk to settle down, then he came back in and fixed the carpet. Jesse said I had done better than she would have, she would have at least raised her voice to Jacob. I was standing right there and heard them both.)

   At that time, she also informed me that Respondent had dropped out of counseling on his own. (The real fact is Brenda and I were going to Marriage Counseling with Dr Jones at the Pendleton Mental Health Department. One day Brenda got so angry with me telling Dr Jones the whole truth that she literally started hitting me on the right shoulder with her fist and left his office. That's why when I had to go back as ordered by Washington State, I went to Dr Jones again, he had counseled both Brenda and myself in Marriage Counseling and was sitting right there across from us when Brenda started hitting me on the shoulder with her closed fist. I didn't stop, Brenda stopped and wouldn't go back.) I got the impression that he continued in counseling only long enough to make it look good for the purpose of our resolving the visitation issue discussed above. Brenda also informed me that Respondent continued to have a very violent temper (If I really had such a violent temper, why did Brenda continually drop all the Restraining Orders?) and that she did not feel that Jacob should stay there for the rest of the weekend. (It's amazing no one else ever saw me hitting on her or any bruises or any other indication of any violent temper I had, except her family and what family would not call the police when that really happens? So, where are the police reports or the ambulance or hospital or doctor bills or anything like that? That's because there wasn't any.) I was scheduled to meet Respondent at McDonald's restaurant in Bend to pick Jacob up, on July 12, 1992. Because of Brenda's telephone call, I made the decision to go to Stanfield to try to check on the welfare of Jacob and to retrieve him.

   After checking with the police and Children's Services Division, I discovered that because no direct 'abuse' had been observed against Jacob, they could not enter the home and remove Jacob from the home. (See? No abuse, even Children Services Division couldn't intervene because nothing was wrong.) As a result, I knew that the only way to get Jacob was to retrieve him myself. I achieved this on the afternoon of July 9, 1992. (Brenda and Jesse took the law into their own hands. If I would have done that I'd have been locked up and we all know that, I'm a man and they are women. This is what I get for being a law abiding citizen.)

When I picked Jacob up, I initially took him to Brenda's parents home. There, I looked him over and discovered that he had many blisters and blisters which had turned to sores on his feet, (If there were really blisters on his feet, Jesse would have noticed the blisters the day before when Jesse met Brenda at my mom's house before they disappeared for four hours going to Children's Services Division and the Oregon State Police in Pendleton trying to pull the boys to begin with and Jesse would have taken Jacob right then, even if it was against the law.) as well as the fact that he was dirty and he appeared to have lost some weight. (As I said, Jacob along with the other boys were playing in the side yard with a chain link fence, a yard contains dirt, they were all bathed every night and clean clothes the next morning and yes, anyone who has a little flab on them, including a child is going to loose a little weight when the flab starts turning to muscle, that's a natural occurrence of the human body. Jacob ate like a horse during that time too, he always wanted seconds, all the boys did. Jacob was very seldom in the house, he was outside playing hard in mom's big yard with the chain link fence around it. To this day, the yard still has that chain link fence around it.) I had weighed Jacob before he left my home for visitation with Respondent and he had weighed 65 pounds at that time. Upon return to my home on July 9, 1992, he weighted only 58 pounds. Jacob also informed me that he had been hit by the Respondent several times in the face during the visit.' (That's definitely not true, if it were, Jesse and all the people in the Main Street Market in Stanfield would have spotted the red marks and/or bruises when Jesse met Brenda before their four hour disappearance act, remember? They both left all four boys with me during those four hours. Now if either of them had really seen or suspected anything wrong, they never would have left all four boys with me for four full hours to begin with. Remember, Paul is still an infant in the little carrier. What really happened is they both got angry at me because I was doing everything right and they didn't have any ammunition against me to let them take the boys back with them. That's what really happened.)

Just after that incident when we were still living in Pendleton and I had graduated from Blue Mountain Community College, it was summer before I started attending Walla Walla College in Walla Walla, Washington. I was packing up my stuff to move out and my mom was helping me as much as she could. All of a sudden Brenda gets angry at me right in front of my mom and starts pounding on my shoulder. I start to put up my hand to defend myself and Brenda runs to the house, picks up the phone and threatens, "If you so much as touch me, I'll call the police." Of course the police would have believed her, she is a woman. So I just got in the car and left. I knew by then it wouldn't do any good to tell the police, I had already tried the Abuse Hotline, remember?

Brenda and I moved from Pendleton, Oregon to Waitsburg, Washington so I could continue with a Bachelor's Degree in Automotive Technology. Well, as the Walla Walla College Transaction Details says. I started school and in the middle of the first semester, Stevey somehow got a splinter in his foot and it became pussy. I took the back of a straight pin and got the splinter out and the puss got on the straight pin. I put the straight pin in the arm of the couch with the pussy side up. I forgot all about the straight pin being on the arm of the couch and when I went to sit down on the couch after getting up, I put the palm of my right hand right on top of that pussy pin, which put the puss inside my right palm. The puss infected my right palm and the infection got so bad my fingers started closing, going closer and closer to my palm as the infection worsened. I couldn't go to school because I couldn't even concentrate enough to read the assignments, not to mention do any writing assignments, I am right hand dominant. I finally had to withdraw from school on October 22, 1992 (Evidence Section Page 48. The adjustment is shown on Evidence Section Page 50 as the official date the withdrawal went through even though the adjustment was backdated.).

I went to a local doctor in Waitsburg, Washington and he gave me a few pills. The pain worsened and my fingers closed tighter and tighter toward my right palm. Brenda finally drove me to the Walla Walla Clinic in Walla Walla, Washington on November 6, 1992 (Evidence Section Page 49.). I couldn't drive any more, my right hand was in so much pain when I tried to move my fingers, the pain was so unbearable I started crying. I saw the emergency room doctor and he started to move my fingers up off my palm and I literally started crying. He immediately went out and in a few minutes came back in with another doctor, a specialist. As the letter from the Walla Walla Clinic states, I started seeing Dr. R and was under his care with my right arm in a sling for 3 to 4 months after the Physical Therapy started (Evidence Section Page 49.). Dr. R. started to try to move my fingers off my right palm as well and when he felt the tension in my fingers, and looked at my right palm, he immediately scheduled me for surgery. I was checked into the hospital the night before the surgery was to take place and the next morning when I was scheduled Dr. R had two emergency cases come in that needed surgery as well. Instead of my surgery being the second one of the day, my surgery was pushed back to the last one that day. The festering of the puss in my palm worsened so much that they had given me all the pain shots they could and my palm was still burning inside. I finally asked the nurse for a wash cloth and a piece of ice. I put the piece of ice inside the washcloth and I had to squeeze the washcloth with the piece of ice in between my fingers and my right palm just to get a little comfort from the burning sensation in my palm. The nurse saw what I was doing and called Dr. R. Dr. R. told the nurse to go ahead and bring me down to the Preparation Room and put me under. Well, when I woke up the operation was over and I had to stay the weekend in the hospital. The following Monday I was released and set up with Physical Therapy for my right palm for three to four months. My whole right hand was bandaged up and my fingers were straight now, but I had no movement in them and no grasp at all. I could feel, but the scars on my muscles and tendons were more damaged than what Dr. R. wanted, it was due to me having to wait all day for the operation instead of being able to get me in when I was scheduled for the operation in the first place. Anyway, my whole right arm was in a sling and my right hand was basically useless. On December 7, 1993 I started seeing

M. M., Physical Therapist as the letter from the Turning Point states (Evidence Section Page 51.). Now, three to four months of Physical Therapy would put it March to April of 1994 of my whole right arm and hand being in a sling while the Physical Therapy was being done on it and then released so I could use my right hand like normal again, right? Well, then how in the world could I have abused Brenda and the boys with my right hand in the sling and little to no movement in my right hand during this time? I had enough trouble using my left hand to eat with. I never made it back to school that January. That incident with the puss in my right hand cost me a whole year's worth of schooling, it started about half way in the Fall Semester and continued clear through to the following Summer. So with that as fact, how could I have done any abuse on any of the boys or Brenda as she claimed I had done?

On December 29, 1992, I filed for a Temporary Restraining Order and had it served on Brenda because the night before Brenda was serving dinner, me and the boys were already at the dinner table. Stevey said something to Brenda that really made her mad and at the time she had a very sharp butcher knife in her hand. Brenda swung around and put the tip of that knife right up to Stevey's throat which scared all of us. Stevey's eyes got really big through fear and I was at the other end of the dinner table with my right arm still in the sling and no grasping power in my fingers. I knew there was no way I would ever be able to make it over the long end of the dinner table and grab Brenda's wrist and still be sure she didn't cut Stevey with the sharp butcher knife, especially with just the use of my left hand. I started talking to Brenda and her attention went from Stevey to me, now the sharp end of the butcher knife was pointed at me, I finally managed to calm Brenda down and she went back to getting dinner. That's why I went in to Walla Walla, Washington the next day with our minister and waited for the judge to sign the Temporary Restraining Order. Usually the Temporary Restraining Order isn't signed the same day it is brought in, but this particular day, the judge wasn't busy so he signed it and it was served on Brenda that night. Brenda was removed by the Waitsburg Police, but it didn't do much good, the very next day, December 30, 1992 Brenda went into the judge, which I might add is against the law, and complained that I am the one who is abusive, the judge pulls the boys from both of us (Evidence Section Page 52-55.). See, now I am a Caucasian Man and I actually did ask for help, twice. What would have happened if I would have been a Mexican or African American? We all know what would have happened if I would have been a woman, I asked for help and was turned away twice. Once in Umatilla County Oregon through the Abuse Hotline and now in Walla Walla County Washington, asking for help didn't do any good. Then counselors and attorneys and society in general wonders why men don't go for help when we are being battered and abused? It doesn't do any good, the system automatically takes the side of the woman and the woman wins. I see all these abuse and battered women shows on television for an hour at a time and at the end of the shows there is a five second, not five minute, but five second statement about how everyone needs to keep in mind there are also battered and abused men in the United States, then the announcers go right back to talking about battered women and children again. If even one time, I would have been able to keep the boys by myself for any decent length of time, I could have proven it to everyone, but no, that was never possible was it. I'm a man, the man is always the abuser. Never, did I ever get a decent chance to show anyone how I could parent my boys. This time the judge sees Brenda when there is supposed to be a hearing and then the determination. The judge isn't even supposed to see the Respondent of the Temporary Restraining Order until the date of the hearing, so how did Brenda get in to see the judge to begin with? Would a man have been able to get in and see a judge like that? No, we would have had to wait for the hearing date and present our defense as the law states. I tried twice to get help and help was never there for me and my boys, in Pendleton I could have went to a shelter by myself, but not the boys. In Waitsburg I had legally served a Temporary Restraining Order on Brenda and she was removed, but then the next day, so were the boys, that's not what a Restraining Order is for, no judge would have done that if the woman served the man the Temporary Restraining Order, the judge would not have seen the man before the hearing date. Brenda had served several Temporary Restraining Orders on me and dropped every one of them before the Hearing Dates up to this point. I could have proven to the judge that there is no way I could have harmed either Brenda or the boys, my hand and arm was still in a sling after my operation. I couldn't even use my right hand at that time and I certainly didn't know how to use my left hand. When I was in grade school if the children tried to do anything with our left hands, the teacher used to smack us on the top of our left hand with a six inch wooden ruler so we wouldn't learn how to write left handed, so I learned everything right handed.

The Dependency Petition was filed and served on me December 30, 1992 (Evidence Section Page 52-55.). I remember that day real well. I made it a point to take the boys into Walla Walla and have a Well Check done on them. Then I called Child Protective Services and told them I had just had the Well Check done on the boys and that's when Child Protective Services told me they wanted me to come to their office, so I went by their office and I was served and the boys were taken from me. I did have a chance to talk to Jan, the Attorney, she had talked to Brenda earlier and according to Jan, Brenda had already laid into her. Brenda told everyone they needed to be on guard just in case I did anything. Well, I didn't have any choice in the matter so I handed Paul to Jan and then Jan said, ok, I have them. Then I saw two Walla Walla Police Officers come out from behind the door and they both looked surprised. I heard one say to the other one, that was easy. I asked what's wrong? Jan said, we were expecting a fight from you according to Brenda you weren't going to let the children go this easily. I told Jan, Brenda says a lot of things to paint a bad picture of me and everyone believes her, then I prove them wrong, but it's always too late. (And don't anyone ever tell me, 'it's never too late.' It's too late to see Jacob or Paul take their first steps. It's too late for a lot of things in the lives of my boys, so don't ever tell me, 'it's never too late.').

James Simma, our case worker told us the fastest way to get Stevey, Jeff, and Paul back was to get with him and he would make up a list of things we both needed to do, once those things were done, the boys would be returned. He also said the fastest way to accomplish the list was if we were to move back in together and work on the list of things as a family. So, the Restraining Order (Evidence Section Pages 57-59.) didn't do me one bit of good, there was no protection for a man and children (and there still isn't). So, in order to get the boys out of Foster Care, Brenda and I move back in together again. Now remember everyone, I'm still working with my fingers on my right hand at home getting my tendons back to where they are supposed to be for movement in my fingers. When I was working with my fingers I could take my arm out of the sling and do my Physical Therapy, but after that my right arm was in the sling, even then I still couldn't use my fingers or right hand to a normal usage and I still had very little grip.

We both went to The Center for Sharing (Evidence Section Page 56.), they were having a class for Parenting Skills. As you can see, The Center for Sharing had already had a class before I started to go, we both completed that with no problem, during the time we were going to these classes, Brenda had met a woman named Polly who was going through her own divorce. Polly's husband's name was Kirk, he was from Thurston County Washington. Kirk had been having an affair on Polly with another woman named JoAnn. Somehow Brenda managed to meet Kirk and JoAnn as well, I don't know how because I wasn't there. It was through Kirk and JoAnn that Brenda met Will.

On February 2 1993 the Agreed Findings on the Dependency Hearing (Evidence Section Page 60-67.) was that Brenda: 1) Receive psychological evaluation and treatment, if needed. 2) To attend parenting classes (6-8 week review). 3) To attend counseling/family therapy. 4) To attend anger management classes and/or 5) To attend homemaking skills classes. 6) To participate in Tot-Spot. 7) To participate in other 'personal' improvement activity of both of their choices. I was to: 1) Receive psychological evaluation and treatment if needed. 2) To attend parenting classes (6-8 week review). 3) To attend counseling/family therapy. 4) To attend anger management classes. 5) To participate in Tot-Spot. 6) To participate in other 'personal' improvement activity of both of their choices.

On February 22, 1993, in Brenda's own handwriting (Evidence Section Page 68-72.), Brenda makes out a Responding Affidavit for me to Jesse. You read page 2 paragraph 2 and the second sentence of the Affidavit states: "All three children were never abused, harmed, or neglected in any way while they were in my care. They were always dressed in clean clothes in the morning and in clean pajamas before bed and after a bath every day. They always had three balanced meals a day, plus nutritious snack between meals. They all played outside during the warm weather and stayed inside on days it rained or the wind blew to hard." Now Brenda is agreeing that there never was any abuse, neglect or harm done to any of the children when Brenda and Jesse kidnapped the boys from my care at my mother's house in Stanfield last July. Remember? Brenda was at the center of attention again.

In March of 1993 Brenda and I sat down together and made up a Final Order for a Parenting Plan (Evidence Section Page 72-81.). In 1.1 the Final Order states it is 'proposed by both parties.' 2.1 PARENTAL CONTROL: Brenda checked: 'The father and the mother has engaged in the conduct which follows: 'A history of acts of domestic violence as defined in RCW 26.50.010'. (1) or an assault or sexual assault which causes grievous bodily harm or the fear of such harm.' 2.2 OTHER FACTORS: Does not apply. 3.1-3.8 SCHEDULE FOR HOLIDAYS: What I want everyone to notice, in all this is 'OPEN VISITATION', Now in 3.13 OTHER: 1) The parents shall have JOINT CUSTODY of the minor two children.' Look at these papers real carefully. There is not even a trace of Brenda believing I am abusive, neglectful or in anyway 'an unfit parent', and this whole thing is made out in Brenda's own handwriting and at the end you will even see her signature on it. As you will also notice, I never did sign it. In other words, I never did say Brenda was a 'fit parent', nor did I agree with the 'Open Visitation' for Brenda. When this was made out Brenda was living at the YWCA in Walla Walla, Washington. I remember one time during all this while the boys were in Foster Care that Jeff was delivered to us at the Child Protective Services Agency Office without any shoes or socks and his front upper tooth was blackened. What is wrong about no shoes or socks is that it was still winter, and there was a little snow covering the ground. I literally took off my shirt and wrapped it around his feet and carried him into the building with my left arm where it was warm and I wasn't going to take a chance on dropping Jeff. I asked the worker where his shoes and socks were and the worker just said the Foster Parents couldn't find them. Then I asked about his blackened tooth and the case worker said the Foster Parent said Jeff was on a sled and the sled didn't stop and he caught his mouth on the rear bumper of the pickup, accidents do happen. I knew right then the boys were not being taken care of too well. Again, I had to get back together with Brenda for the safe of the boys. At least then I had a fighting chance to protect the boys where in Foster Care I couldn't do anything at all to protect them. I was really upset about what the Foster Parents did to Jeff, no shoes or socks with snow outside and a blackened tooth and I couldn't do anything about it.

On April 2, 1993 (Evidence Section Page 82-83.) Brenda needs the 'Spot Light' again and in her own handwriting writes a letter to Jesse's Attorney. As you can see all the way through the letter Brenda wants to be the 'Spokes Person' and fight for Jacob. Brenda makes sure Jesse's attorney knows Brenda is going to be handling my case, it's stated several times in the letter. Did I object? No. Why not? What better Spokes Person can anyone have than the one who is actually instigating all the fights, separations, and lies to begin with? They know what they had planned out and who they used to do their dirty deeds better than any other person on the face of this Earth, including the ones they did the dirty deeds to. Brenda would have been the best person fighting for me I could have had as long as she did fight for me in the court room and not against me. Brenda is the one who called Jesse in the first place and started this whole mess by telling Jesse all the made up lies, remember?

On April 20, 1993 Jesse's attorney writes a letter to me and as you can see in paragraph 2, She was going to object to Brenda handling my case. That took Brenda out of the 'Spot Light' again. So what does Brenda do? You'll see.

On June 15, 1993 the boys were returned to us (Evidence Section Page 85-91.).

On June 16, 1993 we get the evaluation from Carmine, M.A. (Evidence Section Pages 92-95.). When my mom read this, she almost crapped her pants. Why? This is why. Under the Family History it says, Walter has denied any history of being physically or verbally abused by his parents. (This is true, I never was.) However, he states that his father is an alcoholic (the word 'is' means my dad is still alive, my dad died in 1982. This is the very reason my mom allowed me to put a copy of my dad's Death Certificate in this Book (Evidence Section Page 96.) (My dad had been dead and buried for 11 years before this. My dad died before me and my first ex-wife, Jesse, ever got married. Jesse and I were engaged at the time and Jesse attended my dad's funeral with me. Dad was not an alcoholic.) and that his brother does smoke pot (My brother was already working at the Oregon State Correctional Facility in Pendleton, Oregon for several years and later transferred to Twin Rivers Correctional Institution in Umatilla, Oregon when it was first built. He had to be able to pass a 'drug test' before he was ever hired for the Correctional Officer Position. He's been in that position and higher for several years now. The only time he ever even tried any drugs that I know of was while he was in the Navy back in 1972-1978, that's 25 years ago at the time this evaluation was done. My brother learned to be a Nuclear Electrician and had signed up for a six year term. Now how could he be smoking pot in 1993 when he had already been a Correctional Officer for the State of Oregon for several years before this? They have to 'tinkle' in a bottle every six months to keep their jobs, don't they?) His parents are currently separated (I hope to tell you my parents were separated, my mother is still alive even to this day. What is my mom supposed to do, join my dad in his coffin when she is still alive? I'd hate to think that one spouse has to die with another one in order for them to still be legally together. Do they actually have to share a coffin together or something?). with his father retired. (After 11 years of being dead my father was probably pretty well decayed. I guess if someone wanted to call him 'retired', he certainly wasn't working any longer.). During Walter's childhood he noticed his father often 'knocking around his mother' (This is definitely not true.) when he was drunk (As much as I think about this, to this day I can't remember my dad ever being 'drunk' and 'angry', when dad did drink he was actually easier to get along with. There is only one time I can ever remember my dad ever getting angry and he wasn't drinking at that time either. One morning right after my dad got sick, someone started yelling at my mom in our own home and dad kicked them out for raising their voice to my mom, dad was protecting his wife and children. Dad was still very sick when that happened.) Walter stated in written form that he was raped twice by family members. (The question about family members was, 'Have you ever slept with any members of your family?' I said, 'Yes.' and put that in written form. Who hasn't slept with a member of their family? The word, 'ever' means from the time you were born to the present, even when you were an infant you slept with your mommy, she may not have slept, but you fell asleep in her arms several times. I remember when I was still a little boy in my jammies, you know the ones with the little footsies in them? I had to watch out for the 'Boogie Man', remember him? I didn't want the 'Boogie Man' to get me. I would sleep with my mom and dad both, right between them. When it was thundering and lightening outside I'd run from my bed and make sure they knew I was sleeping right between them that night, they didn't have a choice in the matter. I had my back toward my mom and just touched the back of my dad's night shirt, for security, making sure the 'Boogie Man' or the 'thunder and lightening' didn't have a chance to hurt me. I knew if something tried to get me, my dad would feel my little tug on the back of his shirt. My little tug was supposed to wake him up and he would make sure I was safe. I was between three and six years old then. When I was about six or seven, I graduated to my 'blankie' to keep me safe. When my mom and dad took all of us camping or fishing at Jubilee Lake in Oregon, we used to sleep with each other all the time. We had two tents, one for the men

(I was a big six year old man.) and one for the ladies (Linda was a big three year old lady.), we all slept together in those two tents. Mom was in one tent with the ladies and dad was in the other tent with me and my brother, we were the only men in the family. The older kids had their own separate sleeping bags, I don't know about my younger sister, Linda, I assume she did what I did. My dad had a double sleeping bag and I would crawl inside it with my long johns and my wool socks on to keep my feet warm. Dad would roll to one side and I would roll to the other side and eventually my cold feet, even with those wool socks on would find their way to the back of my dad's feet for added warmth. He always said, 'God, you've got icebergs for feet.' Eventually my feet would warm up and I would go to sleep. I might also note here that the next morning, I was the last one out of bed, that sun had to be up and the air outside warm before I would leave that sleeping bag. I was always 'cold blooded' that way. Was there ever any 'sexual dealings' with any of us? We never even though about such a thing. That's why I never thought anything about this question being of any 'sexual nature' when he asked, 'have you ever slept with any member of your family?' And I said, 'yes.'

Now Brenda on the other hand, I know she had been sexually molested by her brother for several years before her mom and dad ever became Foster Parents in Umatilla County Oregon, that was long before I ever met her. She told me that, her brother told me that, and Brenda's own father told me that before he died. Her brother's excuse was that he had learned about sexual orientation in school and wanted to experiment, so he experimented with Brenda. Under Psychological History. Walter explain that he found his wife in bed with another man (This is true, my first ex-wife, Jesse.). He explains that he entered the room and that though he didn't see the man, (This he messed up. I did see the man walking out of our bedroom zipping up his pants and Jesse came out buttoning up her shirt.) he knew that they were having sex (This is false, I was in 'denial' for three years saying she would never do anything like that against me.). He now regrets having left the room without knowing who the man was. Examiner asked why that was the case and he stated 'so I could get him.' (Let me tell you counselors something right now, if it's wrong to want to protect your wife and family, then I'm guilty. Part of that protection is 'beating the crap' out of any man who is 'trying to screw around with his wife'. I know it takes two to tango, but it's also a scientific fact that it takes 'suggestions', 'touches', and 'flirting' to get a woman aroused where all a man has to do is think about it. She should have put a 'stop' to it, I agree, but that still didn't give either of them the right to 'do it', especially in our own home, in our own bed, and with our son in his crib in the same room they were 'going it' in, and then to make-up another reason for her to divorce me. You are lucky I didn't say, 'beat the crap out of both of them', but I was raised not to hit women.) he admits to having significant problem in the past with substance abuse that has included beer and marijuana (Substance abuse? I tried one hit of marijuana in 1977 on my Senior Sneak and that was enough for me.) He denies receiving treatment specific to substance abuse or dependency. (They should make a dependency program for nicotine addiction, that would make more sense. One 'hit' off a marijuana cigarette on a Senior Sneak and I'm dependent on it? I don't think so, that doesn't even make any sense, that was sixteen years before I even took this test, that's a really weird 'dependency'.) Under Criminal History: However, it is important to note that Walter is currently being investigated for 4th degree assault against his wife (I didn't even know anything about this at the time.), after an incident where he reportedly struck her with a closed fist. This has been documented according to Deputy Brown in Waitsburg by one of their children. Deputy Brown also reports that the neighbors are frequently complaining of loud noises and at a minimum verbal fights between Walter and his wife. It is also important to note that Walter's wife is currently unwilling to press charges even though physical evidence of being assaulted is present. (Brenda and I started arguing one day and Brenda ran to our ministers house right across the lot from us. Doris Douglas, our minister's daughter, stated under oath in Circuit Court in the Umatilla County Court House when Jesse and I were in court, that Brenda went in the Douglas's house all hysterical and Doris couldn't get Brenda to settle down, so Doris slapped Brenda a couple of times across the face and that left a bruise. Brenda reported that I hit her with a closed fist and left the bruise, then Brenda refused to press charges against me, Brenda didn't want to press charges against me because Brenda knew that if she did press charges for that bruise on her face that Doris would come forward and tell everyone what really happened that day and how Brenda really got that bruise.)

Brenda started checking into having a 'breast reduction' during this time. I did go to one doctor's appointment with her and heard the doctor tell us both that a lot of women who do have breast reductions are 'victims of childhood sexual molestation'. Being a man, I'm not in the habit of buying women's undergarments, but I bought one bra for Brenda and that was the first and last time I ever spent $50.00 on a bra. I know the straps kept cutting into her shoulders, I also know she couldn't feel anything with her breasts when we were in the bedroom together.

It so happened that Kirk and Polly's Divorce Hearing was coming up and Brenda found out that Kirk and JoAnn were spending the night in a motel room in Walla Walla, Washington so Brenda invited them to come and spend the night before the Divorce Hearing with us. Kirk and JoAnn were to sleep on our living room floor that night. Well, it just so happened that I had to get up and go 'pee' at six o'clock the next morning and Brenda wasn't in bed like she usually was. I started to walk down the hall to the bathroom and heard sounds coming from the living room, now remember, Stevey, Jeff, and Paul are in their bedroom asleep. I peaked around the corner and found Brenda, JoAnn, and Kirk having sex together. They were right in the middle of an 'orgy' with me and the boys in the house, I was somewhat in shock. I went and flushed the toilet so they would hear me and get dressed. Then I went back in the living room and Kirk still had his shirt off and JoAnn had not been able to button all of her shirt up like she usually had it buttoned, she missed a button. I asked Brenda when she had gotten up, she said she, Kirk, and JoAnn got so involved in talking, they talked all night. Brenda never made it to bed that night.

Well, that was enough for me, I couldn't handle anymore, but where would I go and what about the boys? I moved out and Brenda brought the boys over to see me and told me Kirk and JoAnn will never come over again. I'll never talk to them again either. Brenda knew she had been caught 'red handed'. Her apology didn't last too long though, the very next weekend not only did Kirk and JoAnn go to Brenda's house with the boys still there, but they also brought a friend along with them. JoAnn and Kirk introduced their friend Will to Brenda.

This is when I served Brenda with another Restraining Order on July 23, 1993 (Evidence Section Pages 97-107.) and; of course, Brenda couldn't be outdone, she turned around and filed one on me as well (Evidence Section Page 108-110.). I had partially moved out, even though we had Physical Custody of the boys, Child Protective Services still had legal custody and were put back in Foster Care.). In section 1.9, the last sentence reads, 'She even went to the extent of slapping me and shoving me up against the pick-up, I just walked away.' Do you know what the authority who signed the Restraining Order for me asked me before he signed the Restraining Order? He asked if it hurt. I thought to myself, would you have asked a woman that question? Was being shoved up against a pickup supposed to feel good? I finally said yes, it hurt. Then he signed the Order.

On July 23, 1993 my mom writes a letter to the judge (Evidence Section Page 111-114.) for a hearing Brenda and I were going to have. On page 2 at the bottom of the only full paragraph, talking about Jacob, the letter states, 'Only one time he missed a call to his mother was when Walter stayed at my house and Brenda took 4 children, Jacob, Stevey, Jeff, and Paul and accompanied my daughter Linda and her 3 children to the beach to play. On this occasion Jacob missed his only call to his mother to my knowledge. As stated to me by my daughter, Linda, Jacob mentioned his call to his mother Jesse. Brenda's reply was, 'you can do it later.'

On August 2, 1993 Brenda petitioned for a Dissolution of Marriage (Evidence Section 115-117.). I knew something was up when this happened. Did I fight it? Not the Dissolution itself. The last straw for me was when she had her orgy. I knew I couldn't get the boys out, I tried that already and time after time all Brenda had to do was tell everyone I was the mean person and not her, everyone believed her. I love my boys, but I can't fight a bunch of professional idiotic counselors, attorneys, and judges who already have their minds made up.

Well, On October 22, 1993 I found out why Brenda petitioned for the Dissolution. I knew there had to be a reason, more reason than me hitting on her all the time because I knew all those allegations were lies so she could control me. The letter that my attorney for the child custody sent me explained it all (Evidence Section Page 118.). Brenda had found another boyfriend that's why she wasn't trying to come around me. I had a Restraining Order on her and she knew I wasn't going to drop it for the sake of the boys this time. You also need to notice the first paragraph. Child Protection wanted to place the boys with Denise or Tammy, Brenda's sisters. Both Denise and Tammy knew about their brother molesting Brenda all those years before their parents became Foster Parents and before they became 4-H leaders of the 'Hop-Alongs' in Umatilla, Oregon. Anyway, if Brenda's sisters didn't let anyone know about their brother, Justin, molesting Brenda, then why would either sister let the authorities know if Will or anyone of Will's friends or family molested Jeff or Paul? Of course I said, 'NO!' Now finishing that paragraph, 'your wife has a new boyfriend who was convicted (not 'allegedly' mind you, but actually 'convicted') of Indecent Liberties when he was 12 years of age. Although that's been 10 years ago, the Court is concerned that placing the children with your wife at this time would be inappropriate.' At this point, pending the hearing, the children are being kept in foster care. Since I've not spoken to you for sometime, please give me a call and let me know your thoughts concerning next Tuesday's hearing.' While they were in Foster Care I could see them, when they were in Brenda's custody I was too scared to see them because I didn't want Brenda to lie about me any more. Now they were back in Foster Care I could see my boys again. To top this off, I'm not supposed to be angry about this when my boys are right in the middle. Remember? A man isn't supposed to get angry, that's what all the anger management classes tell men.

The boys were put back into Foster Care. Well, on October 26, 1993 the Dependency Hearing came up (Evidence Section Pages 119-125.) and Brenda was supposed to remove Will from the home and put a Restraining Order against him in order to get the boys back. (On page 122 section 3.10 it specifically states that Will is a Child Molester and Brenda is to remove him from her home. Now this order is signed by a judge.) I went through all this and the authorities still wanted me to complete an Anger Management Program. What do you professionals want, Eggs in your Beer? I'd like to see you go through what I went through with your children and not get angry about all this, and don't give me any crap about, 'I don't think that's necessary.' I didn't ask you what you thought was necessary. I made a statement that you do need to go through this in order to understand what you are asking is immoral and inhumane punishment. Child Protective Services gave me a homework assignment, off the record of course. The case worker said if I can prove that Will and Brenda are still seeing each other, then Brenda won't be able to get your boys back and you will more than likely get them. The case worker couldn't promise, but the court would look highly in my favor. So, I had a chance to get the boys back. Well, I got my camcorder out and through the 'grape vine' found out when and where Will worked and I knew Brenda and her parent's vehicles so I watched and waited. I did see their vehicles drop Will off at work, but it was so far away from where I had to hide that I couldn't get a good enough shot because of trees and shrubs, etc. always in the way and Brenda never got out of her parent's van, so I couldn't get a photo or any shot of the two of them together. The two of them were always in the back and the sliding door only opened so far and my ADHD didn't help any either.

Well, Thanksgiving came around and Brenda asked the case worker if she could have the boys for Thanksgiving weekend. The case worker said yes, and I was to get the boys for Christmas weekend, which I never did get. Well, the day Brenda was supposed to return the boys to Child Protective Services, Brenda and the boys never showed up. The case worker had to trace them down and found them in California living with her brother Justin, remember the one who molested her? The case worker called down and talked to Brenda. Brenda told the case worker that her and Will were not coming back. Her brother, Justin, got Will a job where her brother works so they were going to settle there and raise their family there. The case worker had to drive down to California, pick up the boys with the help of the California Child Protective Services and bring them back up to Walla Walla County Washington before the next weekend because that was my weekend to visit my boys. Now when the next hearing comes up, I will get my boys back right? After all, the case worker had to actually go over a state line to get the boys back after they were kidnapped by Brenda and Will. Wrong, I'll skip ahead for a minute.

The next hearing came up and five minutes before the case worker had to leave for the hearing, the Director of Child Protective Services pulled that case worker off our case and assigned the case to someone else. The new case worker didn't know anything about Brenda and Will kidnapping the boys and taking them over the California Border. The Director did it on purpose, Brenda's father called the Director and 'pulled a few strings'.

I had moved back to Stanfield, Oregon by now and started Anger Management Counseling with Dr Jones on November 13, 1993 (Evidence Section Page 126.). He is the same counselor who saw Brenda and I for our Marriage Counseling. According to Dr. Jones, no more Anger Management Counseling was expected to be needed by January 15, 1994.

On December 9, 1993, my attorney for child hearing wrote me a letter stating: "The amount of length of counseling referred to in the Review Hearing Order should be determined by the counselor you are seeing. When your counselor feels that you have received the necessary counseling (or before if he wishes to do so), a report should be provided to me at the above referenced address in order that I can provide said report in the court.' The amount of counseling is left up to the individual counselor. (Evidence Section Page 127.).

On January 16, 1994 (Evidence Section Page 128.) the successful completion of the anger management program through Dr. Jones in Hermiston, Oregon.

On January 21, 1994, I signed a tentative order with the assumption I had my Anger Management Program completed (Evidence Section 129-132.).

Then on February 3, 1994 I received a letter from my attorney for child hearings stating: 'I received your phone message today and wanted to let you know that I had talked to Dr. Brown who had apparently tried to talk to Dr. Jones by phone. He has no problem with what is being suggested, that is that you do your counseling through Dr. Jones (Evidence Section Page 133.). (No one here has any problem with me taking the Anger Management Counseling through Dr. Jones. Now remember, Dr. Jones is the one who Brenda and I went to for our Marriage Counseling, so Dr. Jones was already familiar with our case. Dr. Jones didn't have to start from scratch like any other counselor would have had to do.) However, he would like to talk to him or at least send him a copy of your evaluation before you get started. (Actually I took a copy of the evaluation into Dr. Jones and let him look at it and Dr. Brown also sent Dr. Jones a copy of the evaluation. I showed Dr. Jones a copy of my father's Death Certificate and Dr. Jones started wondering if Dr. Brown had gotten his notes mixed up. I also tried to get a hold of Dr. Brown and show him my dad's Death Certificate, but according to his receptionist, I would have to pay for his time and I would also have to go through the Child Protective Services Division because they were the ones who paid for the original testing in the first place. I didn't have the money to pay for an appointment and Child Protective Services didn't want to hear anything about what evidence I had (Evidence Section Page 135.). In that regard, you need to sign an authorization which you will need to sign which specifically authorizes him to release any and all information to Dr. Jones on your behalf.'(Evidence Section Page 134.).

On March 4, 1994 Dr. Brown changes his mind after he talks to Dr. Jones and finds out I have already completed the program (Evidence Section Page 137.). Child

Protective Services can't allow that, I'm not supposed to get custody of my boys, remember? Brenda's father pulled strings and there is no way Child Protective Services is going to allow me to get my boys from Brenda or Will. The only way Child Protective Services can make sure of me not being awarded custody is once again, change the rules. You've seen the previous court signed papers, they all specifically state, Anger Management and at first the length of the program was up to the individual counselor, then the program was changed to Batterer's Treatment with a minimum of one year with group sessions. Now the program is changed for the second time to Anger Management with the length of one year with group sessions. That makes twice they changed the original order of the court. at least six months after the other one because it's every six months we went in for the placement of the boys. So what I was supposed to take was three different things, the last two were not ordered by the court in the first place. In other words, it took Child Protective Services, the counselors, and the judges over eighteen months to legally get the boys into Brenda's custody even tough the boys could have been placed with me in less than six months. After the first hearing, it was over six months to the second hearing when they changed first ordered because I had completed the first order, then over another six months went by for the second change, that's well over twelve whole months of dead time that Child Protective Services, the counselors, and the judges say doesn't count. I've already paid Dr. Jones for all those hours and according to Child Protective Services, wasted five months in the process while my boys are in Foster Care, yet I'm still not supposed to allow all this to bother me. I'm trying to get my boys back and the attorneys, counselors, and Child Protective Services are wasting precious time writing letters back and forth for over a year, changing the programs that I have already taken because I was ordered to take those programs to get my boys back. The big thing is Dr. Brown had to change his position because Dr. Jones who already had both Brenda and myself in Marriage Counseling said I had completed the Court Ordered Anger Management Counseling, the court didn't order Batterer's Treatment, check the court orders, the first ones all state, Anger Management. Since I was going through Dr. Jones, the program didn't take long enough for Brenda to legally get the boys. Now with Batterer's Treatment with a minimum of one year, Child Protective Services was assured that my treatment would take too long to be able to fight Brenda in a court room. All this going on and I'm still supposed to be able to hold down a truck driving job and drive back and forth for visitation for my boys. Dr. Jones agreed to see me on the weekends and other days I had off, no group meetings can do that, so in order to complete the NEW RULES, it was impossible for me to complete the last one. All the counselors and case workers say, 'they'll let you off work.' Let me tell you counselors, case workers, and judges something right now. Don't assume another person or company will let someone off work just because you say they will. Companies don't always do that, no matter what.

Unknown to me, the Interstate Compact Placement Request was signed by three people, one on April 12, 1994; one on April 25, 1994; and one on June 8, 1994 (Evidence Section Pages 138-139.), and if you notice in the middle the Interstate Compact Placement Request lists the mother and grandfather as the caregivers. In other words, Brenda and her father had Legal and Physical Custody of all three boys (Evidence

Section Page 139.). What is so strange about all this? I hadn't even had my In-Home-Study done yet, there is supposed to be an In-Home-Study done on both parents and then the placement is to be determined, not the placement before the In-Home-Study. My In-Home-Study isn't done until June 27, 1994 and then the In-Home-Study is done by an old neighbor of Brenda's parents and it was also done on the Umatilla Indian Reservation without the consent of the Federal Government or the Indians (Evidence Section Pages 158 second and fourth paragraphs.). Yes, their old neighbor told me that she was Brenda's parents old next door neighbor, but if you object, your objection is legally documented as 'Uncooperative' and you automatically fail the In-Home-Study, so I couldn't object or I would automatically fail the In-Home-Study. What's my point here? The last Interstate Compact Placement Request was done on June 8, 1994. My In-Home-Study isn't done until June 27, 1994 with no chance whatsoever of passing it. The decision as to where to place the boys was done before my In-Home-Study was even done. Jeff and Paul were already placed with Brenda before I even had my In-Home-Study done by Child Protective Services in Pendleton, Oregon.

Now during all this time, I was still watching Will to catch him and Brenda together when Brenda serves me with a Restraining Order in Umatilla County Oregon (Evidence Section Pages 140-152.) and. Will serves me with a Stalking Complaint (Evidence Section Pages 153-156.). Of course when the judge found out why I was following Will the judge dismissed all charges. Remember, Walla Walla County Child Protective Services in Washington told me to catch them together and bring them proof, so during the time I was out with my camcorder, they filed these charges against me and the judge dismissed everything, but before the judge dismissed it all, the Placement and In-Home-Study's were done, it sure looks bad for someone to do that with all these In-Home-Studies and charges pending. Sure Brenda knows that, that's why she does it that way. She knows when everything is scheduled to take place and plans everything accordingly.

On July 18, 1994 there was a Review Hearing Order signed by a judge (Evidence Section Pages 161-168.). Notice in 2.6: the Mother, Will and Brenda are still involved with each other and under 2.10: Brenda is to get a six month restraining order against Will. Under 2.6 the Father: Child Protective Services still has me down as stopping the anger management program that Dr. Jones said I had completed. How can I complete more of what a therapist says I already completed and signed two letters to that effect? 'Other: DSHS recommends the three children be placed with Brenda and her boyfriend, Will. (Now this is the same **Will who is a Convicted Child Molester and Convicted of Indecent Liberties from Thurston County Washington. DSHS is recommending that three young boys be placed in the same house as a Convicted Child Molester and Convicted of Indecent Liberties. Not an Accused Child Molester mind you, but a Convicted Child Molester.**) Hermiston's Children's Services is willing to provide courtesy supervision, and Oregon Interstate Compact authorized placement on July 19, 1994 (Evidence Section Page 169.) Now this is the very next day from when the judge signed the order that Brenda was to get a six month Restraining Order against Will and was to make sure Will was out of her life if she wanted to keep the boys. Now look at this date and look at the date of my In-Home-

Study. The Brenda Home Study Addendum was done on June 27, 1994 and July 19, 1994 (Evidence Section Pages 169-170.) and this one includes Will when right before this Brenda was ordered to put a six month restraining order on him and keep him away from the boys (Evidence Section Page 157-160 and 169-170.). The Interstate Compact Placement Request was done on April 12, 1994 (Evidence Section Pages138-139.). I might also mention that Brenda's Birthday is April 13 the day after the Interstate Placement was done. That is also before my In-Home-Study was even done.) With these records you saw the Interstate-Placement was actually done and arranged before my In-Home-Study was even done. Not only that but the boys were placed with Brenda and Will both living in the same home one day after the judge signed the Order that Brenda was to keep Will out of her life and away from the boys. On July 28, 1994 Brenda and I were finally legally divorced (Evidence Section Pages 171-176.).

The next review hearing (Evidence Section Pages 186-192.) Look at section 2.6.1 on page 183, it still doesn't give me credit for the anger management, in fact it says that I stopped my anger management when they have two letters from my counselor stating I had completed it.

What it really is, is that Dr. Jones is a Christian Counsel also licensed by the State of Oregon and with more qualifications than most doctors in the secular field want to think about. I added Dr. Jones's qualifications in the Evidence Section of this book, you all have read them. How am I supposed to continue counseling with Dr. Jones when Dr. Jones says I am done? Should I pitch a tent in his front yard? I'm not qualified to tell Dr. Jones that I need more counseling. That's like the patient telling the doctor to do a brain operation when all you need is a few stitches in your arm. I didn't stop the counseling, I was finished with the counseling according to the attending psychologist. So I actually did comply with the original court order. And the fact that it took them a year to make up their minds, changing programs all the time, allowing Brenda to get most of her stuff done before I even had a chance to get done, since mine was changed three times.). No where does it mention any longer that Brenda needs to keep the Convicted Child Molester out of her life and away from the boys like the judge ordered just one day ago.

Now look at the ORDER part in 3.4 under <u>Father (Walter Burchett)</u> number 4. Walter to have no contact with the children as recommended in the home study done by Brenda's parents ex-next door neighbor, caseworker for Oregon State. (Now remember, **this caseworker was re-hired by Child Protective Services for these two In-Home-Study's, the one on me, and the one on Brenda and then she was going to be let go again. At least that's what she told me at the time she did my In-Home-Study.**

Now keeping all this in mind, this caseworker over-rules not only one, but two Dr.'s who are Oregon State Licensed Counselors, both of whom are Christians, both of whom used to contract out for Umatilla County Mental Health as well as having their own Private Practice, Dr. Jones is the most recent one who counseled Brenda and me when we were going to Umatilla County Mental Health for Marriage Counseling. You are going to sit there and tell me this caseworker is more qualified to say who is and who is not mentally capable enough to have contact with children and to what extent that contact should be? **According to this caseworker and Child Protective Services in**

Walla Walla County Washington and Child Protective Services in Umatilla and Morrow Counties in Oregon, a Convicted Child Molester is more qualified than a man who has successfully completed not only one, but two separate counseling programs with two separate Christian Doctors who are both Licensed Counselors in the State of Oregon. Before anyone is licensed by the state, they need to have their own credentials from their Professional Organizations, that means the American Counseling Association, the Oregon Counseling Association, and approval from the Federal Bureau of Investigation for counseling juveniles. On top of all this, Brenda was actually ordered by the court to keep Will out of her life forever or loose all the children, remember? **The caseworker also didn't like the idea I was living on the Umatilla Indian Reservation at the time of the In-Home-Study. That means there actually had to be something wrong with the boys or the Umatilla County Child Protective Services wouldn't be allowed to take the boys out of my care because of the Federal Laws regulating County Personnel coming onto the Umatilla Indian Property (Evidence Section Page 158.).** I never looked for a place on the Umatilla Indian Reservation, it was a very nice quiet place the boys could run and have fun, it was fenced in and two fields away from any main roads.).

On November 30, 1994 Brenda writes a letter to my divorce attorney (Evidence Section Page 202.). Notice in the second paragraph, now instead of Joint Custody as Brenda wanted, and wrote in her own handwriting (Evidence Section Page 73-81.), she now wants full custody so Will can adopt them. Also she brings it up that the Court Ordered me to have no contact with the boys because of what her ex-next door neighbor that did the In-Home-Study says, yet Brenda is wanting the court to allow Will to adopt them even though he is a Convicted Child Molester and he was Convicted of Indecent Liberties or I can have supervised visits with someone she has final approval of, which I might add, Brenda would never approve of anyone except maybe one of her sisters who hid the fact that their brother repeatedly raped Brenda for several years before he left home. Brenda's repeated rapes by her brother is the reason Brenda had to have a breast reduction to begin with. Now there is the medical evidence of the rapes, so again there is the control issue of hers.

March 6, 1995, Dr. Jones writes a letter to the judge (Evidence Section Page 203.). In paragraph one, Dr. Jones states he has been in practice for sixteen years as an individual, marriage, and family counselor. Those are some credentials, not to mention all the seminars and workshops he has done. In the second paragraph, Dr. Jones again re-emphasizes he does not believe I have an anger problem and that Dr. Jones actually believes I was misdiagnosed. Now this is not only in black and white, but also in Dr. Jones's own handwriting and notarized by a Notary Public in the State of Oregon. What more could I do? The judges already had their minds made up where the boys were going to go and on top of that I still hadn't had my In-Home-Study done yet.

As far as not having any contact with the boys, there are two reason for that: 1) I started working to pay for all these proceedings, and 2) I have never and will never contact the boys as long as they are in Brenda's, Will's or any of her relatives care. I've had enough of their lies and deception and I'm not going to put up with the lies or deception any longer so I don't contact her, in fact, I don't even know where she lives or her phone number and don't want them. All I know about her is she is living in Umatilla, Oregon and the boys go to school in Umatilla, Oregon. As long as I don't contact her or the boys while they are in her care, she can't turn around and say I said things or threatened to do things when I didn't do either.

She also wants a breaking in period because I had not visited the children for several months. (That's because Brenda had custody and I know how that woman can lie and her ex-next door neighbor made sure I was not allowed any visits thanks to her father.) A breaking in, reacquainting time is needed. (When a child is taken out of their parents house and placed in Foster Care there is no 'breaking in' or 'reacquainting time' the children go through. Don't tell me that a 'breaking in' or 'reacquainting time' is really needed when children are constantly being taken out of their parents' homes and placed with total strangers all the time. As so many counselors both in the profession of counseling and teaching have said to me and millions of other people, 'children are resilient, they will bounce back.' So let them bounce back without the 'breaking in' or 'reacquainting time'. What that 'breaking in time' is really for is for the 'neutral third party' to watch the parent and how the parent acts and re-acts towards the child in different given situations. That's what that 'breaking in' time is really for, it's just a cover-up title for a professional to see how the parent acts and responds to different situations with the child.) This visitation only pertains to Jeff and Paul. Stevey is not the Respondent's biological child. If he (Stevey) wishes to be a part of the visitation, by agreement between the parties, the Court would support that idea.

On June 30, 1995 the Parenting Plan was signed by the judge (Evidence Section Pages 207-214.) and I couldn't do anything about it. I had no income, it's hard to have a job when you are always fighting in court rooms. No one can be in two places at once.

On February 8, 1999, we go to court because Will wants to adopt Jeff and Paul (Evidence Section 215-216.). The judge actually signs the Order for Adoption, what stops the adoption from going through is the In-Home-Study done by Child Welfare Services. Now I ask you, what's going on? Child Welfare, formerly Child Protective Services Also Known As Children Services Division allows the placement of Jeff and Paul with Will and Brenda and now they don't allow the adoption to take place? What variable has changed? Oh, wait a minute, no one believed me and mom about how bad a mother Brenda was and now that I'm out of the picture everyone is finding out I was right all along. Is that it? Yet all the children are still with Will and Brenda and one of the older boys actually snuck out of the house through his window and had to be brought back by the Umatilla Police Department. Another one of the boys, a younger one, was actually hiding behind a locker at the Umatilla School because he didn't want to go home and the police were called again. The Umatilla Police Department have been called in several times and Children's Protective Services have had numerous complains about Will and Brenda, those are just the ones I know about. What a bunch of crappy covering up. Even though the court from Washington said the Convicted Child Molester was to be out of Brenda's life forever or Brenda was to loose the children, period and that was signed by a judge just one day before the boys were actually placed with Brenda and Will with the help of Brenda's ex-next door neighbor and her father. The children are still in the possession of Will and Brenda.

I had a chance to see Brenda's dad just before he died. Brenda brought him over to mom's house where I was staying. He was hooked up oxygen at the time and knew he wasn't going to live much longer. I flat out asked him why he helped Jesse and Brenda kidnap the boys and then helped Will and Brenda kidnap the boys the second time and how in the world they got out of any charges. Brenda's dad just said she's his daughter, and he did make a few phone calls and talked to a few people. I asked him if he knew what he did. I told him, "I will never have any say in how my own boys are being raised because of you. I had all the evidence I needed plenty of times and for one reason or another the evidence was never accepted or the programs I was supposed to complete were always changed. I can't keep asking my mom for a thousand dollars every time we turn around. The last time we went to court was my last chance to be with my boys because we can't afford it.' He said he never thought of it like that.

Now Will and Brenda still have my boys, and from what I understand Child Protective Services has been called in several times because of the neglect to them, among other things. I don't have any idea why Child Protective Services haven't pulled all their children out of their house yet. **Now, this is really what it's like to be an abused man fighting for your children's safety and welfare. Now you may understand why more men don't come forward that have been abused, it doesn't do any good.**

Just about a year before I decided to move to North Dakota I started receiving letters from an old friend of mine from North Dakota. At first I ignored her letters because she was married. Nine months later mom and I was approached by Brenda to see if we wanted to join a bowling league with the boys at Desert Lanes Bowling Alley in Hermiston, Oregon. We joined just to be around the boys one night a week for the summer. During that time I had both boys ask me if they could spend the night with me and mom and I had to tell them it was ok with me, but I knew Brenda would never allow it. I also saw Will and Brenda disciplining the boys and I watched how the boys reacted to a lot of different things. I know the boys are not as bad as Brenda lets on. The boys are being punished for no reason. Just about the end of the bowling season, I finally had a decision to make and my old friend was still wanting me to move back to North Dakota. I knew the only way to prove to anyone about what I was saying to be true was to literally move completely out of the state and away from the situation. That was the only way I could prove I was not the one causing all the problems. How could I cause any problems when I'm not around? Why did I visit the boys at the bowling alley when they were on league? Because I knew Brenda and Will couldn't lie about what I was doing when there were a lot of witnesses around.

CORINNE

CORINNE

During the time mom and I were bowling with the boys, Corinne and I were talking over the internet. She tracked me down somehow and after a year of her sending me letters through the mail, she found my email address. I usually deleted them, but once I figured out there was no way to prove that I wasn't the one abusing the boys until I was totally out of the area I started talking to Corinne again. Corinne and I actually met at some kind of church gathering many years ago. We wrote back and forth for over a year while she was still attending Minot High School and I was in Stanfield, Oregon. We were actually engaged through the mail, then she married someone else, from the Air Force Base. She started telling me about her husband going out on her and one day in particular he went to a Nudist Camp on her birthday, they were living in Naples, Italy at the time. Her marriage was already broken up, she wanted me to get back together with her even though she was still married to another man. I'm not in the habit of breaking up marriages, and I didn't like the idea of coming back to Minot, North Dakota for a married woman, but she kept insisting on it. Finally I gave in and came back to Minot and she got a divorce. I told her before I left Oregon that I had back problems, but she didn't care.

When I got to Minot I went into Vocational Rehabilitation to see if they could get me on some program. Vocational Rehabilitation found out I had a Bachelor's Degree in Psychology and two minors, one in Counseling and one in Religion. I had also completed one semester in a Master's Program for Counseling school age children up to the age of eighteen. Vocational Rehabilitation was going to send me back to school for Refresher Courses in that area. They also found out I had been in counseling before and asked me to sign some Release of Information Papers, so I did. Then Vocational Rehabilitation wanted me to go through one of their own classes for Addiction to Alcohol.

I really wasn't addicted to Alcohol, but that's ok, I went anyway. This particular class was to last for six weeks two nights a week. Well, everything went good until the fourth week. See, that's usually the strategy, they let you get about half-way through the classes, then if they don't like your answers to how you see things, they kick you out and put down on their reports that you quit. You'll see what I mean.

Dean was the instructor for this class. On the second night of the third week Dean asked me why I didn't participate more in class discussion. I told him that he wouldn't like my answers. He asked me what I meant. I told him, he keeps on talking about a man and woman who are husband and wife being 'their own person', but if the husband or the wife gets some king of Sexually Transmitted Disease, would he sit there and tell me their spouse won't get that Sexually Transmitted Disease as well, when they are intimate because they are 'their own person'? Or if the husband or wife signs a contract with a bank and their spouse stops paying on the note then the bank won't come back to their spouse because they are 'their own person'? That doesn't even work in Divorces after the judge signs the Divorce Decree stating who is to pay what bills. The creditors will always go after the ex-spouse for their money if the one who is actually supposed to pay the bill stops paying it for any reason all. Then the husband and wife are definitely not 'their own person', but 'one flesh' now aren't they. Are you going to sit there and tell me that if a man comes up to your wife and gives her a very passionate kiss you won't be angry, hurt, or upset? Or if she accepts that kiss and returns another very passionate kiss to another man that you wouldn't get angry, upset, hurt, at the man and your wife? Are you going to sit there and try to tell this class you wouldn't care one way or anther? Husband an wife are 'one flesh', you know you would get upset if you found your wife was being romantic with another man or you don't love her, that's part of being 'one flesh', not 'your own person'.

Dean asked me to leave the class, then at break asked me to stay, so I stayed. In the second night of the Fourth week, Dean asked the class another question. Yes, I remember what the question was because I was asked to leave the class for the second time with my answer. Dean asked who has been the biggest helper in the classes lives going through all our troubles. There were a lot of women in the class and most of them said the same thing, their children. Then it was my turn to answer the question, I said, 'Jesus is my biggest helper.' He has gone through everything with me. I don't have children to help me through things. In fact, your children shouldn't even be helping you through these things to begin with. Your children are to rely on you, not you relying on your children. A helper means you rely on them. The helper is supposed to be strong enough to be able to support their own needs and your needs as well. Children have enough problems just being themselves, not to mention having to take on adult responsibilities. My helper is Jesus Christ of Nazareth. He is strong enough to handle all of His needs and mine both.'

Dean asked me why I couldn't leave Christianity outside the door when I came to class. I said, 'No, I can't. He is in my heart just like the love you have for your wife is in your heart. Can you leave that love outside when you come in here? No, you can't. Then Dean asked me to leave the class again and this time he didn't ask me back.

With Corinne having to work and me not being able to work, we did a lot of verbal arguing. She was angry that she was the only one working and I just got kicked out of the class I needed t get the few classes I needed to get my career started. She had every right to be angry about that. I couldn't work at any job that required me to lift over 10 lbs by order of the Back Specialist. With Dean asking me to leave the class the second time that was too much for us. With Corinne being a Cold Christian herself, she understood that I couldn't leave Jesus outside the door like Dean wanted me to, but that didn't help matters much (If you don't know what a 'Cold Christian' is get my book called, MATTHEW'S WORD 'TWO': REAL WORD OF GOD BIBLE, it explains in detail the difference between a 'Cold Christian' and a 'Backslider', my other book called, 'HEAVENLY ANGEL LAY LAY EXPLAINS THE DIFFERENCE BETWEEN A 'COLD CHRISTIAN' AND A 'BACKSLIDER' also explains the difference. Corinne finally wanted to talk to Brenda and somehow found her phone number. (That's something I really dread having. If I had my way about it, my ex and I would not have either phone number or address.) That's when things really changed for the worse.

I started going to Cottonwood Lake, I think that is in McHenry County, around central North Dakota to get away from the hitting until the sheriff told me I had to leave. Even when I told the sheriff Corinne was hitting me, he still made me go back to her. A lot of friction started up between Corinne and I, then one day she blew up on me and I had her arrested. Now she is about 5' 2" and abut 275 lbs and I'm about 5' 9" and about 185 lbs with a herniated disc in my back. That's why I'm not supposed to lift over 10 lbs.

One day she went overboard, she took her finger nails and tried to pull my ears off my head, so I called the police. The Minot Police Report in December 2003 (Evidence Section Pages 217-223.) shows what happened and tells how it happened. She was charged with Simple Assault which was later reduced to Disorderly Conduct. I can't remember if it was Officer Jack or Officer John that did the questioning before she was arrested. Anyway, one of them asked me if I did anything to her. (As you can see by the police report, she didn't have a mark on her. I knew better than to do anything.) I looked at the officer and asked him, this one question, 'If I was a woman would you have asked me that question?' He looked at her and said he was afraid they were going to have to arrest her. I thought to myself, 'What do you mean , you're going to have to arrest her?' If the man would have hurt the woman like she hurt me, you would have him in handcuffs already, no questions asked.

There are several times she fell to the floor faking being passed out so I would give her attention. What made me catch onto that is when the police started to arrest her and she fell to the floor right in front of them.. I panicked and started to help her like I usually did. The one of the police officers said, no, if she needs help, we'll just call an ambulance for her. She immediately got right up to her feet with no problem. She had been faking passing out to get my attention all this time. I finally had her evicted from my home in May.

I filled out a Grievance Form for Vocational Rehabilitation and was sent a Request for Client Assistance services that's dated February 1, 2005 (Evidence Section Page 224.). I know it may be difficult to read so I am going to type in what I wrote in as my grievance.

It reads: "I was asked to leave the Alcohol Treatment Program by Dean. Then he puts in my file that I quit treatment. I didn't quit, I was asked to leave the Alcohol Treatment, he told me to leave. Vocational Rehabilitation says it's considered Disrupting the Flow of Discussion when I bring Jesus up in the conversation. If they don't want His name brought up then they shouldn't ask me who is helping me with staying sober. I'm not going to leave Jesus at the door. A lot of people talk about how they are saying sober for their children. How their children are first in their life. Jesus is first in my life. Counselors didn't want me Cold, when I was drinking. Now they don't want me Hot when I am sober talking about Jesus. The want me Luke Warm, sober not talking about Jesus, that I refuse to do. Scriptures say, Revelations 3:16, 'So then because thou art Luke Warm, and neither Cold nor Hot, I will spue thee out of my mouth.' 1 John 2:2 'Whosoever denieth the Son, the same hath not the Father: he that acknowledgeth the Son has the Father also.' Luke 12:8, 9, 'Also say unto you, whosoever shall confess me before men, him shall the Son of man also confess before the angels of God. But he that denieth me before man shall be denied before the angels of God.' I also refuse to go to anymore women counselors period, or men counselors because they are not wise counsel according to the Word of God. Luke 7:30, 'But the Pharisees and lawyers rejected the counsel of god against themselves, being not baptized of him.' You can not have wise counsel without Jesus. You need Jesus in the room in order to have wise counsel. I refuse to give up my Heavenly Birthright for a bowl of lentles. Your forcing me to leave Jesus outside is also against my Constitutional Rights as United States Citizen.'

A letter from Phil tells me to get in contact with Mickey, Director. March 16, 2005 (Evidence Section Page 221-222.) Mickey, the Director takes his time in getting back to me for the grievance. What all this amounts to is Vocation Rehabilitation closed my case because I wouldn't start the Alcohol Treatment Program again from scratch (Evidence Section Page 230.). I was willing to meet them half way and finish the last week, two more sessions, but no, they wanted me to start the whole treatment program from scratch again, just because THEY KICKED ME OUT!!! I can see where that would be going. Every time I get close to the end of the six week training program they would tell me to leave and then want me to re-take the program again from scratch and don't even think about telling me I don't know that would happen. I know that would happen just as well as I know I'm sitting here typing this on my computer and so do you, so don't even go there, it won't work. Jesus is training me now in a brand new career, business and authorship. The Nazarene has a way of turning things around for His glory.

Most recently in July of 2006 I called the Federal Bureau of Investigation here in Minot, North Dakota and talked to an agent. He told me the investigation would have to start in Walla Walla, County Washington for the kidnapping charges and in Umatilla County Oregon for all the abuse, neglect, and crossing the Federal Line to do the In-Home-Study on the Umatilla Indian Reservation. So I called them (Evidence Section Page 231.).

On July 24, 2006 I wrote a letter to Child Protective Services because I heard through the grapevine that there was sexual activities going on in the home of Will and Brenda and the sexual activity wasn't between Will and Brenda in their bedroom either (Evidence Section Pages 232-233.).

During that time I also wrote a letter to the Umatilla School District requesting a copy of all of the boys' work and also gave the Superintendent a copy of the Oregon Revised Statute (Evidence Section Page 243.) that states right in the statutes that I have every legal right to do so (Evidence Section Page 234.).

On August 6, 2006 I wrote a letter to Children, Adults and Families, Child Welfare (Evidence Section Page 235-236.). I told them about the kidnapping and Brenda being molested by her brother all those years.

On August 7, 2006 I wrote another letter to the Superintendent of the Umatilla School District in Umatilla, Oregon (Evidence Section Pages 237-240.) and had him share this information with all the boy's teachers. These things are things I learned over the several years I had attended school and college. This was before I knew Brenda had held them both back so many years and had the boys labeled as Mentally Retarded now. When I found that out I was very angry. Remember, I had been with them just a few years back and had a chance to observe them first hand. I also had learned that the professionals have wanted to put them in a Live-In-Institution in Pendleton, Oregon to find out if there really was anything wrong with them and Brenda keeps denying them access to the boys.

On September 14, 2006 (Evidence Section Page 241.) I requested all the papers for the boys with my legal right to receive the papers to find out what was really going on (Oregon Revised Statutes Evidence Section Page 243.). I know there have been several complaints about Will and Brenda and can't seem to find out why they have any children in there home, not just my boys.

On October 30, 2006 (Evidence Section Page 242.) I write a letter to my oldest son in the Umatilla School District and have a staff member read it to him.

On January 8, 2007 I write a Power of Attorney (Evidence Section Page 244.) and attach a copy of the Oregon Revised Statutes (Evidence Section Page 243.) along with the letter that Brenda wrote to my mom (Evidence Section Page 245.). The Power of Attorney over-rides any and all letters or requests that Brenda could make because it's the law. I transferred all my powers as the non-custodial parent to my mom through the Power of Attorney and the Oregon Revised Statutes says I have that legal right to obtain any and all information without Brenda's say so or knowledge.

Oregon Revised Statutes 107.154 Effect of order granting sole custody of minor child to one parent on authority of other parent:

Unless otherwise ordered by the court, an order of sole custody to one parent **shall not deprive the other parent of the following authority:**

(1) To inspect and receive school records and to consult with the school staff concerning the student's welfare and education, **to the same extent** as the custodial parent may inspect and receive such records and consult with such staff. (This means I can talk to the staff, get the boys papers, grades, anything I ask for the school is to give to me and without Brenda's knowledge, unless the school contacts me when Brenda talks to such staff and receives such papers. That's what 'To the same extent' means.)

(2) To inspect and receive governmental agency and law enforcement records concerning the child **to the same extent** as the custodial parent may inspect and receive such records.

(3) To consult with any person who may provide care or treatment for the child and to inspect and receive the child's medical, dental, and psychological records **to the same extent** as the custodial parent may consult with such person and inspect and receive such records.

This means exactly what it says, **"to the same extent"** means no one contacts me when she gets any of these things and by this ORS, they are legally bound not to contact her when I receive such records or talk to such people or professionals about the boys. Legally, I don't have to go through Brenda to talk to, receive any papers ,or reports, or consult with any professional, about my boys.

On March 30, 2007 I write a letter to Justice Wallace in the Hermiston Court (Evidence Section Pages 246-250.)

ADDITIONAL

INFORMATION

AND CONCLUSION

ADDITIONAL INFORMATION

The next pages in the book cover a conversation I had with Brenda and Jan. I wonder how does Jan know all this in the first place? Jan is Brenda, that's how. These are things that only someone close to the case would know about. Look at the dates on the one from Jan it's dated March 20, 2007 on Lulu.com (Evidence Pages 251.). She gave a review on Lulu.com before she ever emailed me pretending to be a college student. Then she wanted everyone to read the actually court documents. As far as reading the actual court documents, good idea. That's exactly what I wanted everyone do to. That's also why all the court documents and other evidence was included in my original book WHAT'S WRONG WITH THIS PICTURE? Brenda put up such a fuss that the book was pulled off the shelf. If she wasn't guilty of what I was saying about the actual court documents, she wouldn't have wanted it pulled off the shelf so much. This is why I had to split the original book up into two different parts. The first part is the Events Section and the second part is the Evidence Section. Now the Evidence Section still contains all the actual court documents as well as all the things in Brenda's own handwriting and her signature as well. That section of the book lulu.com has no control over, that section can only be found on my website www.crossover-ministries-publishing.com and that will not be pulled by anything less than a Federal Court Order.

Then the next ones you will see from Jan pretends to be a college student who emailed me dated March 19, 2007 through May 9, 2007. Let's take March 19, 2007 first. Jan talks about doing a term paper for college and wants an abused man's view point as well as a woman's. Notice she says her paper is due the end of the term, that's the end of May. Look at the dates on the one from Jan it's dated March 20, 2007 on Lulu.com (Evidence Page 251.).

To answer the question of why I never called or visited the children (Evidence Section Page 256.). I always have to go through Brenda to see or even talk to them and Brenda is always there, and having her or another member of her family or friend there, then no, the scale is way too far out of balance with that arrangement. The police can't even get to the truth because Brenda is always there, the police have to question the boys with her present. What abused woman wants to have to go through their abusive ex-husband? None, so why would an abused man want to or even be ordered by a court of law to go through his abusive ex-wife? That is why I don't contact the boys when I have to go through Brenda. When they were in Foster Care, I always visited them on every day I had.

Now, lets go to April 18-20, 2007 and May 8-9, 2007, (Evidence Section Pages 252-259.), from the email. Why is Jan so concerned about what the law says in this particular situation? She is only a college student, or is she? The law says you have to have someone's permission to quote them and use their name when they are talking to you person to person, like in journalism. When you have the actual court documents, those court documents are public information and their consent to use their full legal name and quote what that legal document says is completely legal. Why is it legal? Because it's public information. How did Jan know that I used the real names in the book in the first place? I never stated in the introduction they were the real names of the people and according to Jan, that's all she had to go by. Another thing Jan mentions is me using the real name of Will being convicted for Indecent Liberties from Thurston County Washington (Evidence Section Page 254.). Those papers weren't in the Introduction of the book either, so how did Jan know anything about that?

As far as the Indecent Liberties and Convicted Child Molestation facts go, those facts are also on legal documentation and his full legal name is used on those documents as well (Evidence Section Pages 118 and 122.). Those legal documents were actually given to me by the authorities and my attorney who received them from Children Protective Services in Walla Walla County Washington who received them from Thurston County Washington because Brenda and Will would not stop seeing each other after Brenda was warned several times. My copy of those papers at that time became public information because Will and Brenda did not obey the authorities. The second one was signed by a judge in Walla Walla County Washington. That's also why Brenda and Will kidnapped the three juvenile boys and took them over the Oregon/California Border, then when contacted by Child Protection of Walla Walla County, they refused to bring the boys back.

On April 19, 2007 Jan comes back and says her professor moved up the date the report was due from the end of May to the 11th of May (Evidence Section Page 252.). Now I have been going to school a long time and have had a lot of professors, a professor won't do that, especially when that paper is a major portion of the student's final grade for that class. Then after I wouldn't answer her questions before the hearing in Hermiston that my mom had to go to, Jan got really snotty.

On April 20, 2007 (Evidence Section Page 252.) I ask Jan for the school she is going to and the name of her professor to verify her story, this she refused to give me. Why wouldn't Jan allow me to have the professor's name and the name of the college? I'm not asking for her phone number, but her school's, where I can talk to her professor. That is a good way of verification. I could have called her school, listened for the receptionist name the college and ask for the professor. If what Jan was telling me was true, she would have had no reason to deny me that information.

On May 9, 2007 Jan writes back and claims her professor finally extended the deadline for the paper back to its original date, the end of May (Evidence Section Page 258.). Again, I'll tell you, I have been going to school a long time and have had a lot of professors, a professor won't do that, especially when that paper is a major portion of the student's final grade for that class.

Also on May 9, 2007 Jan tells me if I don't want to give her my side of the story, she will contact the others in the book and get their side of the story (Evidence Section top of Page 259.). There is only one thing wrong with that idea. I never mentioned their last names in the story section of the book, and especially not in the introduction section of the book, their last names were only on the evidence in the Evidence Section of the book and Jan said she couldn't afford to buy the book, therefore she could not have had any information about anyone's last name, except mine and my mothers. My ex wife's last name was changed when she married Will. On May 9, 2007 (Evidence Section Page top middle of 259.) I replied to the remarks on Lulu.com and told Brenda I was onto Brenda's little fishing trip pretending to be Jan. There are so many Red Flags in her emails it's not funny. Not to mention the language she and her sisters used, that part I did white out. There is no reason to include vulgarity or profanity in the book.

On May 9, (Evidence Section Page 260.) my first reply on Lulu.com. I waited until after the May 8, 2007 hearing for a reason. I'm sure everyone is wondering what hearing I am talking about. Well, when the boys almost died because of overdoses of the wrong medications the specialists prescribed to them due to the false symptoms Brenda told the specialists the boys had. (The specialists have wanted to put the boys in a Live-In-Care-Facility to keep them for a while and observe them to see what, if anything is really wrong with them and Brenda has always refused.) So I made out a Power of Attorney and signed my legal rights over to my mom for her do to some leg work and see what was going on. The Power of Attorney is not in the book, the book was published around November of 2006, the Power of Attorney was not made out until January of 2007. So how did Jan or Brenda know anything about the Power of Attorney in the first place? Brenda finds out about the Power of Attorney and my mom going to the Umatilla High School to leave notes for my son for the staff to read to him, letting him know my mother and I are thinking of my boys. Brenda gets angry and puts a Restraining Order and a Stalking Complaint against my mom. Now we are talking about a 76 year old great grandmother who has been a resident of Stanfield, Oregon since I was in my crib, that's 47 years ago. My mom's picture is on the back of this book to give everyone an idea of what my mother is capable of and what she would do and not do.

A Restraining Order is if someone hits or threatens to hit you, my mom never hit any of my boys, in fact, just the opposite. One time Jeff hit Brenda and my mom wrote a note to Jeff telling him not to hit Brenda anymore, that's how my mom is.

On May 9, 2007 (Evidence Section Page 261.) Brenda writes a review on Lulu.com. Brenda starts talking about the evidence and the Power of Attorney. Brenda claims the non-Custodial Parent does not have the rights to the children's papers, medical or legal records or anything else the Custodial Parent has. Well as you have all seen in the Oregon Revised Statutes, non-Custodial Parents do have that right, and without the Custodial Parent knowing anything about it, and Brenda has seen it as well. It's in the school file of the boys and Brenda has read that, so Brenda knows it's legal as well. Brenda continues, about alleged abuse, well, you will see later on in the evidence that her sister claims to have taken her to the doctor's office when I allegedly threw her down the stairs during her pregnancy. Now if I had thrown her down a flight of stairs why would her sister have to take her anywhere, especially when her sister lived in the Hermiston area with her husband, while Brenda and I lived in Pendleton. How do I know where we lived? That is the only time she fell down any stairs, I know that according to a neighbor woman who heard her fall down the stairs and took her to Dr. Sheep's office, after I had drove off in our car like Mental Health told me to do.

Brenda says I don't have any legal rights to find anything out (Evidence Section Page 261.) so the Power of Attorney is not any good (Evidence Section Page 261.), but I have already showed you with the Oregon Revised Statute a few times now where a non-custodial parent does have those rights and I don't have to go through Brenda to get anything, so the Power of Attorney is legal and binding. Oregon Revised Statutes 107.154 states:

Effect of order granting sole custody of minor child to one parent on authority of another.

Unless ordered by the court, **an order of sole custody to one parent shall not deprive the other parent of the following authority:**

1) To **inspect and receive** school records and to consult with school staff concerning the child's welfare and education **to the same extent** as the custodial parent may inspect and receive such records and consult with such staff.

2) To **inspect and receive** governmental agency and law enforcement records concerning the child **to the same extent** as the custodial parent may inspect and receive such records,

3) To **consult with any person** who may provide care or treatment for the child and to receive the child's medical, dental, and psychological records, **to the same extent** as the custodial parent may consult with such person and inspect and receive such records.

4) To authorize emergency medical, dental, psychological, psychiatric, or other health care for the child if the custodial parent is for practical purposes unavailable or,

5) To apply to be the child's conservator, guardian ad litem or both.

Now with the Power of Attorney (Evidence Section Page 244.) I made out and gave to my mother, transferring all my legal authority to her until I came back to Umatilla County Oregon, my mother did and still does have all these rights listed above. With the Power of Attorney my mother is just the same as it were me right there requesting information and receiving all the paperwork and files of my boys myself. So at the time my mother did and still does have all those rights because I haven't returned to Umatilla County Oregon since I made out the Power of Attorney. In all actuality, if the officials don't honor the Power of Attorney and allow my mother all these legal rights, they are actually breaking the Oregon Revised Statutes Law. As long as professionals and schools do not contact the non-custodial parent when the custodial parent gets information from the school or other professionals, then those school or professionals are actually breaking this law if they do contact the custodial parent when the non-custodial parent wants all this information. That is the meaning of 'to the same extent' and that is in black and white. So Non-Custodial Parents do have that right, and without the Custodial Parent knowing anything about it.

A Stalking Order is for someone who is out to kill someone else. Going to the school to leave a messages and talk to the Umatilla High School Staff is far from Stalking anyone. In fact, look on the back cover of this book and you will see my mom's picture. I asked her for her picture so I could put her picture there to let the readers know she is not a person to hit or stalk anyone, especially children. In fact, my mom is a volunteer for the school districts in Umatilla County to help the teachers teach the younger children. The month before the May 8, 2007 hearing for the Stalking Order,

Brenda drops the Restraining Orders right when court starts and the cases are dismissed. The Stalking Complaint was the May 8, hearing and why I wouldn't talk to anyone about my book called WHAT'S WRONG WITH THIS PICTURE?, until after that hearing date., the judge dismissed that as well. Brenda didn't have any grounds for serving it on my mom in the first place.

On May 9, 2007 (Evidence Section Page 261.) Brenda says I threw her in the snow and she got a 103 degree temperature when she was nine months pregnant. If that were true there would be a hospital bill and doctors reports, not to mention Child Protection stepping into the picture. Anyone living in the Hermiston or Pendleton area knows we didn't get any snow drifts big enough for any person to land in. There aren't any snow drifts that high until you get into the mountains on the East side of Pendleton over Cabbage Hill. Certainly not enough snow to give anyone a 103 degree temperature. If that really did happen and she really did have a 103 degree temperature, then where are the medical reports and where is the ambulance call? There isn't any because it never happened. Neither boy was born pre-mature. Both boys were born at St. Anthony's Hospital in Pendleton, Oregon and none of this so far has happened in Walla Walla County Washington or in Waitsburg, Washington where we lived when I was attending Walla Walla College in College Place, Walla Walla County, Washington.. Now, that area may get a few inches of snow all winter long, but none that accumulates all winter long. So what snow drift is she talking about? None, because it didn't happen.

On May 9, 2007 (Evidence Section Page 261.) Brenda also says the boys were born with bruises on them that I caused when I beat her up. Anyone with any smarts knows that if a child is born with bruises on them other than what happens during the birth by a licensed Physician, the children are automatically taken and placed in Foster Care with a full legal investigation, well the boys were never placed in Foster Care in Pendleton, Oregon or in Oregon period for that matter. That didn't happen until we moved to Washington and that was in Walla Walla County, and neither boy was born in Washington, they were both born in Pendleton, Oregon in Umatilla County before we moved to Washington for me to continue in my Bachelor's Degree in Automotive Technology at Walla Walla College in College Place, Washington.

Now with all that said, Brenda goes on and threatens not only me, but the State of Washington as well (Evidence Section Page 261.). What is so interesting is that she never disputes the file is accurate, just that it was obtained illegally which means the file is accurate and did happen. Not only does she not dispute the Premeditated Felony Kidnapping is accurate, she actually tries to make up a reason for the Premeditated Felony Kidnapping. As I have said several times, my copy of the file is totally legal to use and I have also told everyone why it is totally legal. Brenda goes on to deny any connection between herself and Jan. You can tell by what is being said and the attitude of Jan, that Jan is Brenda.

Tammy, Brenda's sister comments about the pictures on the front and back of the cover of WHAT'S WRONG WITH THIS PICTURE? She is under the assumption that I said the damage shown in those pictures were done when Brenda and I were together, you can tell she never read the book. The book explicitly states in the section about my ex-girlfriend the damage to me was done when I was seeing her, not Brenda, that damage was done in Minot, North Dakota. I am so specific about that I even included a copy of the police arrest record of my ex-girlfriend at the time the damage was done.

Then Tammy says Brenda had a miscarriage. Tammy never lived in Pendleton, Oregon, her and her husband always lived in the Hermiston/Umatilla area closer to her dad and mom who lived in Umatilla, Oregon so how could Tammy have taken Brenda anywhere including to Dr's Sheep's office which was located in Pendleton, OR. That just doesn't make any sense, they say I pushed Brenda down the stairs which I didn't, but if I was at home at the time, then I would have taken Brenda to Dr. Sheep's office myself, that just goes to show you I wasn't even around, the neighbor lady took Brenda to Dr. Sheep's office after Brenda fell down the stairs on her own. I was already gone for a drive just like the counselors at Mental Health told me to do. Another point of information, Tammy didn't even know how to drive back then. She definitely didn't have a drivers license or a car. By the way, for anyone who doesn't know the area, it would take a good 45 minutes to drive from Hermiston to Pendleton, if they were in Umatilla then it would take closer to an hour for the one-way drive to Pendleton. If you are in Umatilla, you would have to drive through Hermiston on Highway 395 and then through Stanfield to hit the freeway, then another 25-30 minutes to get to the first Pendleton exit. Where we lived it was the second Pendleton exit you would have to take to get to Brenda, then you would have to drive through a little traffic to take the right hand turn going up to our townhouse. Yes, its that far away, so if the neighbor lady hadn't taken Brenda to the hospital, Brenda would have called an ambulance, not her sister who was about an hour away. Now you can see why it would be totally stupid for Brenda to call her sister to go clear to Pendleton to take Brenda to the Dr's office. Tammy didn't even know how to drive back then, she definitely didn't have a drivers license or a car.

Tammy even talks about her going down to California to pick up all three boys. First of all, what government agency is going to send anyone to do anything for that agency? There is no insurance, no funds for gas, no funds for payment, no authority to get the California Child Protection to pick the children up. Tammy didn't even know how to drive back then, she definitely didn't have a drivers license or a car, remember? When Brenda and I met, Brenda didn't even have a drivers license, I had to let Brenda drive with me and go for her driving test after we met. It just doesn't make any sense.

The only time I know of that Brenda may have had any miscarriage is when she forgot to take her 'birth control pills' in the middle of her cycle and started taking them again after that. She came out of the bathroom one day and told me she had a miscarriage and had flushed it down the toilet. Tammy threatens to use some of her own 'pull' against me just like her dad did before. Tammy actually accuses me of hitting her, now if I would have hit anyone I would have been arrested on the spot.

By the way everyone, this is the same sister that gave her first-born son to her mom and dad for adoption. You want to talk about abuse, lets talk about the times that their dad hit Tammy's first-born son she gave to her mom and dad to adopt, every time her dad didn't like the way the son was acting, the dad would take his cane and hit the boy on the top of his head, that happened in public and private both. This is the same dad who pulled some strings for Brenda to get my boys out of foster care and keep her out of being charged for three counts of Premeditated Felony Kidnapping.

The big question about California is, how did a six year old, a three year old, and an infant get down to California to begin with? Don't forget, the six year old is supposed to have ADHD as Brenda points out to a letter to Jesse's Attorney when Brenda describes the boys she left with me, the three year old and the infant are supposed to be Mentally Ill. How could a six year old have taken himself and the other two younger boys, one still in an infant carrier from Umatilla, Oregon down to California in the first place? Tammy and Brenda's stories just don't make any sense. Everyone reading this book knows that would never happen in the first place, Child Protection would send a worker down to pick up the boys, not some relative of the minor children. Also Brenda goes into Will's files being sealed and wonders how I got access to his sealed files (Evidence Section Page 261.). Also on that same page Brenda not only threatens me, but the State of Washington. Brenda states and I quote, "This juvenile record was obtained illegally and the State of Washington and Walter will pay for it." (Evidence Section Page 261.). Now if that's not a threat, I don't know what is. As I have said a few times already, the reason Child Protective Services made sure I had a copy of Will's juvenile record was because Brenda did not get Will out of her life when she was told to several times, and ordered to by the judge, now my copy of the portion of his juvenile record Child Protective Services gave to me is public information. Brenda also thinks the boys do not have a choice in who they want to live with after they turn 18 years old, even though they are listed as handicapped now and are legally able to go to public school until they are 21, they are still legally the age of majority at 18, and they still have that legal right go wherever they want. They don't even need a judge's order at 18 (Evidence Section Page 261.).

Brenda never disputes the juvenile file is accurate, just that it was obtained illegally, nor does Brenda dispute the fact that Brenda and Will kidnapped the boys out of the Walla Walla County Foster Care and took the three boys down to her brothers in California without the legal authority to do so, and against the wishes of Walla Walla County Foster Care in Walla Walla, Washington while the boys were with her on the Thanksgiving Holiday Weekend. Brenda goes on to deny any connection between herself and Jan. You can tell by what is being said and the attitude of Jan that she is Brenda.

On May 10, 2007 Brenda actually confesses to kidnapping the boys and taking them over the Oregon California border when she didn't have legal custody of them. I quote Brenda as saying, As far as kidnapping, Washington decided not to because I wasn't running from them, I was running from you to protect my kids from the monster you are." (Evidence Section Page 263.) and the boys almost dieing twice when she won't allow the professionals to give them 'In-Care-Treatment' like the professionals have wanted to do for a long time now. I want the FBI involved in this case. I actually called the FBI and asked them to get involved in this case, but they won't get involved in a case except for two ways. The first way is the local officials call the FBI in, or two, the public makes enough phone calls to the local FBI in that jurisdiction that the FBI listens to the public and gets involved in a case. In this case it would be to the FBI covering Walla

Walla County Washington and Umatilla County Oregon.. Walla Walla County Washington FBI because that's where the boys were in Foster Care when Brenda and Will kidnapped them. Umatilla County Oregon FBI because that's where the boys were residents at when they almost died and my first son was kidnapped and the judge signed the adoption order for a Convicted Child Molester to adopt my boys. Not one time did Brenda ever say she wanted the FBI involved in this case because she knows what would happen when they do get involved. Now you see why the only law enforcement agency that could cover this case is the FBI, and the local officials should have called them in several years ago. Now my quote back to Brenda, "Brenda, there was no reason to run from me when you kidnapped the three boys. They were in Walla Walla County Foster Care and we were separated, you were seeing Will at the time and Will was supposed to be out of your life because of his past criminal record. You and Will had it all planned out to have a new life with your brother's help until CPS came down and picked up the three boys. At that time I was back in Stanfield, Oregon living with my mom, so there was no reason for me to be around you and no reason for you and Will to kidnap the boys. Nice try. You just admitted you did; in fact, kidnap the boys from Walla Walla County Foster Care and took them over the Oregon/California Border for no reason." (Evidence Section Page 264.). Another note of information here, this happened before Walla Walla County Child Protective Services told me to follow Brenda and Will to get proof that Brenda and Will was still seeing each other. It was before I found out Will's past history, but apparently not before Child Protection told Brenda they knew about Will's past history as a Convicted Child Molester, Convicted of Indecent Liberties and to remove him from her life or she would never get the boys back.

On May 10, 2007 (Evidence Section Page 263.) now Brenda is insinuating one of the boys was found playing on the highway. When she left and went to her women's retreat with the Salvation Army in Pendleton we lived out in the country in a mobile home and it was a good 100 feet uphill from the highway. There was no mention of any of the boys playing on the highway because they never did play on the highway. We all played in the yard, on top of the hill. Now just stop and think about it, if she was gone then how can she know anything that took place during that particular weekend in the first place? She can't, she is making it up as she goes. Brenda goes on and says she lost a child because of me. As I said before, the only child I know of that she lost was because of the miscarriage of her missing her 'pill' and starting them again. I had nothing to do with that (Evidence Section Page 263.). There is no ambulance calls, no doctor reports of a miscarriage due to beatings, no children taken away while we were in Umatilla County Oregon, nothing. Why isn't there any proof of any of this taking place? Because it never happened in the first place.

On May 10, 2007, (Evidence Section Page 264.) I answer the letter from Brenda about her and Will kidnapping the boys and taking them over the Oregon/California Border. In the letter I explain why there was no reason for her to run from me and the judge couldn't have dismissed any charges because no charges were ever filed. The District Court Judge in a county doesn't have the authority do dismiss a Felony Charge, no matter what Felony the Charge is. In this case it's three counts of Premeditated Felony Kidnapping because it was planned. It would take a Federal Judge to dismiss those charges and that would be done only after there are charges filed and the arrests were made. There were no charges filed because her dad pulled some strings to keep her and Will out of the Federal Pen. That's why the case was transferred over to another case worker five minutes before the old case worker had to leave for court that day, the new case worker didn't know any thing about the kidnapping or who Will was or even his background or conviction.

A copy of my Washington Counseling Association Certificate of Membership (Evidence Section Page 265.).

CONCLUSION

There is a term in Psychology called, 'Stereotyping'. Once I was stereotyped by Rhonda and Jesse, without the money to fight the allegations in court the stereotyping continued. It became so bad that no matter what I said or did, if Jesse or Brenda stuck together, no official would believe me or my mother and it was just the two of us that was always around. There was a Psychology Study done on 'Stereotyping". You see there was a Doctor of Psychology who was teaching the subject of stereotyping in a university and the instructor gave his students an assignment to go out and pretend to have certain characteristics that a particular person would have if they had such and such wrong with them. With each student the instructor gave a different illness and symptoms to pretend. Then the instructor also told each student to keep his name and phone number handy and when the student was done with the experiment the student was to call the instructor and the instructor would vouch for the student's release from the mental hospital and explain to the doctors in the mental hospital the students were doing all this for a class project. While the students were 'committed' to the hospital the students were to make notes and write in a journal each day, sometimes several times a day. Well, what happened was once some of the students, unknown to the staff at the hospitals, were committed and the students began to take notes, the staff started talking back and forth saying, 'yep, that's what he/she has alright. See, they are doing everything the DSM IV says a person with that particular illness would do. All of a sudden the staff is confirming what they believe these students have when there is actually nothing wrong with the students to begin with, just because someone else told the medical doctors something was wrong with these students. Once a diagnosis by a professional doctor is made on a person it's tremendously hard, very costly, and extremely time consuming for anyone to prove the professional doctor made a mistake, even with other professional doctors in the same field disagreeing about the diagnosis. One in particular student in the above real events at the university actually had to hire an attorney and go to court to get released. The doctors in the mental institutions blamed the instructor because the doctors in the mental institutions weren't informed about any class that would deliberately stereotype their students with a particular illness, when in all actuality the students were as sane as anyone else. So the instructor said, 'Ok, next semester I'll call you and let you know when I start sending my students out so you will be aware of them coming. See if you can spot the students then.' The doctors at the mental institutions said, 'Ok.'

The next semester rolls around and the instructor didn't make any phone calls to the mental hospitals, but all of a sudden there are people coming into the mental institutions wanting to be checked in, claiming this symptom and that symptom and the doctors in the mental institutions start calling back and forth, saying to themselves, 'Wait a minute, this is one of 'so and so's students, we caught him this semester.' The doctors in the mental institutions started sending real people who needed treatment away thinking the real people with illnesses were the students who were being sent out. Finally the doctors in the mental institutions were so proud of themselves about catching all the people they thought were students and sending them back to the instructor they just couldn't help but call the instructor and tell him they knew he was sending the students out again and they had sent all the students away. The instructor said, 'I decided not to send anyone out this semester. That's why I didn't call you.' The mental health doctors in the mental institutions were actually sending away people who really needed help.

Between Jesse and Brenda conspiring all the time between the two of them and lying all the time, all the Restraining Orders that Brenda served on me and later dropped before the court hearings even came up, Doctor Brown messing up his notes, Brenda's father pulling all the right strings, Jenny Carr, Brenda's ex-next door neighbor, being re-hired by Children's Services Division for this particular case, Walla Walla County Child Protective Service covering up Will and Brenda kidnapping Stevey, Jeff, and Paul and taking all three boys over the Oregon/California State Line, having a case worker drive down to California to pick up Stevey, Jeff, and Paul to bring them back to Walla Walla, Washington just before my next visitation. Then still giving the boys to Brenda who was molested by her brother Justin for several years, and Will who is a Convicted Child Molester, Convicted of Indecent Liberties. Let's not forget Jane, Jesse's attorney from Bend, Oregon who helped Brenda and Jesse get this whole ball rolling. Between all of them, I never even had a chance to keep Jeff and Paul from Will and Brenda. Not even with two private psychology doctors, saying there was nothing wrong with me, both of whom worked with the Umatilla County Mental Health Department and one actually counseled Brenda and I in Marriage Counseling. Doctor Jones not only put everything in his own handwriting, but also notarized the letter to the judge. The judge didn't like the letter from Doctor Jones because the letter wasn't done on a letterhead. I don't know about anyone else out there, but if a doctor has written something in their own handwriting and had it notarized before a notary public, I'd accept that a lot faster than a type written letter done on any letterhead. A typewritten letter done on a letterhead can be made on any computer. With a handwritten notarized letter, you know that letter is done by that particular doctor. No notary public is going to risk a huge fine or any jail time for anyone. The huge difference is the Notary Public and their signature stating under oath the doctor is the actual person who signed their name to that letter and that letter can be verified by any handwriting expert. Once my stereotyping started, there was no stopping it no matter what professional I hired or what I did. Now, with my training and schooling, the American Counseling Association, the Washington Counseling Association, and the Federal Bureau of Investigation all say I'm 'ACCEPTABLE' to counsel school age children. A man can't be considered 'unfit' with his own children and be able to live with or marry some other woman and be considered 'fit' to raise or help raise her children, that just doesn't make any sense. That means it's not really the man who is 'fit' or 'unfit' now doesn't it.

I tried getting even the basic information from drug stores. You know, the doctor's name, address, phone number and prescription of the boys. The drug store wouldn't give me anything and actually called Brenda. Before I even got home, Brenda was calling me wanting to know what I was wanting and told me I could come to her. That's like the abused woman going to the abusive man for information. A woman wouldn't want to do that, neither did I and I still don't. I know about the law and the protection clause, but the information of the doctors name, phone number, and prescription for your own children is not going to give the custodial parent's address or phone number away. The information about what is prescribed to the child and the child's attending physician is not illegal to give to the non-custodial parent, in fact it's the law that you are supposed to give that information to the non-custodial parent unless it's ordered by the judge not to. All you need is the Divorce Decree and the proper identification to make sure there is no Permanent Restraining Order on the non-custodial parent to keep that information away from the non-custodial parent. You can always call the court house to make sure you are reading the latest Divorce Decree or the Parenting Plan. The information where the custodial parent and the child live and the phone number is protected, if it's written in the Divorce Decree or Parenting Plan. All you drug stores and all kinds of children's doctors need to start obeying the law. The non-custodial parent doesn't need to hire an attorney or go to the custodial parent when it's legal for the non-custodial parent to have the information without the custodial parent knowing. The Oregon Revised Statues is in the Evidence Section of the book shows that clause, it says, **'Unless ordered by the court, an order of sole custody to one parent shall not deprive the other parent of the following authority: (3) To consult with any person who may provide care or treatment for the child and to inspect and receive the child's medical, dental and psychological records <u>to the same extent as the custodial parent</u> may consult with such person and inspect and receive such records'**. The agency or business doesn't notify the non-custodial parent when the custodial parent or the doctors do something for the child or get information and neither do the professionals who give their services; therefore, the drug stores, or doctors are actually breaking the law when they notify the custodial parent when the non-custodial parent wants information about their own child. This is what **'to the same extent'** means. If you don't like the law then change it, but don't break it. I tried getting help three different times, twice with Brenda that is documented and once with Corinne that isn't documented. Yet no governmental agency helped a Christian Caucasian Abused Man, this is why men don't come forward when they are being beaten up, it doesn't do any good. The Salvation Army did try to help, but Brenda tracked me down. As of November 2006, I finally heard from Child Protective Services in Pendleton, Oregon, they want money to get a copy of the file, to this date, July 2007, I still don't have that file. After three months, the Umatilla School District in Umatilla, Oregon finally did send me a copy of all the papers of Jeff and Paul's records.

Child Protective Services <u>has been called several times by other people in Umatilla County</u> about Will and Brenda, but the children have never been put in Foster Care yet. Either that or I was never notified about it, which by law, I was supposed to be. When someone actually figures out how Will and Brenda still have custody of Jeff and Paul, still living in Umatilla, Oregon along with other children in their home. You let me know, will you? Another thing, I am still ordered to pay Child Support every month. The court has ordered me to send money to a Convicted Child Molester and an abusive ex-wife to raise my boys. If anything bad is happening to Jeff or Paul, I had to pay for the gas to get Jeff and Paul there to begin with.

As far as women telling the men who have children: I've heard a lot of women say, "Well, I've pretty much raised my kids. But I suppose I could raise another kid or

CONCLUSION   Page 67

two." If a woman said that to me, I'd drop her like a hot potato, her attitude stinks. That's like saying she is doing him a favor. First off, you aren't raising his children, he is allowing you to help him finish raising his children. There is a big difference. Second, you are not doing the man a favor if he is interested in you that much to bring up the possibility of allowing you to help him finish raising his children. Her attitude needs to be, "I'd be honored to help you finish raising your children." Do ladies think the man is doing the lady a favor when he helps her finish raising her children? Or is she allowing him to help her finish raising her children out of respect and trust? Helping someone finish raising their children is an honor, not a favor. One more little note here. As many times as I have been cheated on, I can honestly say, I have never cheated on anyone. I did have offers, but always turned them down. Sometimes I wished I hadn't turned the offers down, but to this day I still believe I made the right choice.

I only have one thing to say and this statement is especially directed toward any and all Convicted Child Molesters in the United States of America. Not just the Accused Child Molesters, but the actual Convicted Child Molesters. If you want to settle down and be around children of any age, go to Umatilla County Oregon, Morrow County Oregon, and Walla Walla County Washington, the governmental agencies will place children with you, help you get legal custody of children, judges will actually sign the adoption papers for you to adopt the children. Child Protective Services and the judges may even allow you to be a Foster Parent. The District Attorney's won't even prosecute you if you take a child over the state lines. You have everything working on your side in these three counties. The same Child Protective Agency which is over Umatilla County Oregon is also over Morrow County Oregon. This book exposes **A CORRUPTED SYSTEM OF CHILD PROTECTIVE SERVICES, THE JUDGES, A CONVICTED CHILD MOLESTER, A CHILD MOLESTER WHO HAS NEVER EVEN BEEN ARRESTED YET, AND AN ABUSIVE WOMAN.** The corrupt legal system in four different states, Oregon, Washington, California, and North Dakota. Wouldn't you like to know if there is a Child Molester or someone Convicted of Indecent Liberties is living beside you? Conclusion? No, the Conclusion hasn't happened yet. **THIS IS WHAT IT'S LIKE TO BE AN ABUSED MAN.**